GW00362058

INDEX
ON CENSORSHIP

INDEX ON CENSORSHIP 1 2001

WEBSITE NEWS UPDATED WEEKLY

www.indexoncensorship.org
contact@indexoncensorship.org
tel: 020 7278 2313
fax: 020 7278 1878

Volume 30 No 1 January/February 2001 Issue 198

Index on Censorship (ISSN 0306-4220) is published bi-monthly by a non-profit-making company: Writers & Scholars International Ltd, Lancaster House, 33 Islington High Street, London N1 9LH. *Index on Censorship* is associated with Writers & Scholars Educational Trust, registered charity number 325003 *Periodicals postage*: (US subscribers only) paid at Newark, New Jersey. Postmaster: send US address changes to *Index on Censorship* c/o Mercury Airfreight International Ltd Inc., 365 Blair Road, Avenel, NJ 07001, USA
© This selection Writers & Scholars International Ltd, London 1999
© Contributors to this issue, except where otherwise indicated

Subscriptions (6 issues per annum)
Individuals: Britain £39, US $52, rest of world £45
Institutions: Britain £44, US $80, rest of world £50
Speak to Tony Callaghan on 020 7278 2313
or email tony@indexoncensorship.org

Index has made every effort to discover copyright owners of material in this issue. Any errors or omissions are inadvertent

EDITORIAL

Private grief and public memory

'It is too early, perhaps, for a Truth and Reconciliation Commission, but something like an Historical Truth and Political Justice Committee would be appropriate.' This is Edward Said, proposing one way out of the terrible impasse between Arabs and Jews, between Palestine and Israel. But how can this be done when, as Avi Shlaim indicates (p50), there is no common narrative; when what each side remembers is totally at odds with the other? *Index* explores the relationship between memory and history, between rival versions of events, acknowledging the uneven, complicated and halting process that marks our assimilation of the past.

Frank Kermode reflects on the modern psychoanalytic assumption that 'repression is simply a way of seeming to get rid of things by keeping them' (p87). But what of cultural repression, and its connection with the reconstruction of political events? Rachel Whiteread's extraordinary monument to the Holocaust, playing havoc with the symmetry of Vienna's Judenplatz, is, as Hella Pick reports (p56), one of the signs that Austria is perhaps abandoning its collective repression and beginning to look at its past. And though we tend to think of memory as redemptive, we are always, unavoidably, confronted with its selective nature. Alessandro Portelli's story of the massacre at Fosse Ardeatine (p67) is a dramatic case in point: memory turning culpability on its head, blaming not the Germans for perpetrating the massacre but the partisans for their 'irresponsible attack'.

'All over the world, commemorations of atrocities have turned into memory wars.' Stanley Cohen's essay (p40) takes a fresh and thought-provoking look at the ongoing debate on whether collective truth-telling must always lead to judicial accountability. There are international criminal proceedings such as those at Nuremberg and the International Criminal Tribunal for Rwanda, trying to identify those responsible and bring them to justice. Truth commissions, on the other hand, are set up so that wrongdoing can be described, acknowledged and the frame of public memory changed.

The fact is that the task of creating a shared memory and a consensus about the past is riddled with problems. The undeniable power of the mothers and grandmothers demonstrating in the Plaza de Mayo in Argentina (p168), and now in the streets of Algiers (p27), is that they understand the importance of confronting denial with private remembrance, by naming the names and showing the photographs of their 'disappeared' in a public place. ❏

contents

Facing page, far left
*Dome of the Rock, Jerusalem, 1991:
riot police break up a demonstration.
Credit: © Judah Passow / Network*

*Other images on these pages are
captioned in the articles*

letters

False science

It is necessary to correct a number of errors and falsehoods in Jon Entine's 'Breaking the Taboo' (*Index* 4/00). Entine claims that it is an 'uncontroversial scientific conclusion' that the achievements of black athletes can be explained by genetics. Nothing could be further from the truth. The available scientific evidence is contradictory and ultimately inconclusive. Few credible biologists or geneticists give any credence to Entine's claims in his book *Taboo: Why black athletes dominate sports and why we're afraid to talk about it.*

Entine's suggestion that he has tried to decouple the link between racial intelligence and physicality would be the book's only saving grace, but again this claim is false. In fact it has only served to *strengthen* the dubious statistical correlation central to white supremacist doctrines for over a century. Philippe Rushton, a notorious racial scientist, endorsed Entine's central thesis on a recent BBC television programme, claiming that intelligence was linked to brain size, which affected the pelvis shape of mothers trying to push out clever babies with big heads, meaning that they could not run fast as they then had odd-shaped legs (*Black Britain*, BBC2, September 2000). Thus we apparently get clever Asians who can't run, blacks with little heads, low IQs, but good skeletal shapes for running, and with whites, of course, the norm from which we can measure the 'deviant' performance of the non-white 'races' of the world.

Placing Entine alongside figures such as Marqusee, Hoberman and Whannel gives the impression that his book is a serious scholarly tract fighting censorship for the greater good of knowledge, truth and justice, rather than a skilful piece of ideological rhetoric which is actually full of factual errors, statistical sleights and non-sequiturs. *Taboo* should still be debated and discussed of course, but only in the same critical way we would *The Bell Curve*, the journal *Mankind Quarterly* or Gobineau's *Essai sur l'inégalité des races humains.* ❏

Ben Carrington is co-editor of 'Race', Sport and British Society *(Routledge, 2001)*

Paedophilia

It is not always a simple matter to distinguish the right to freedom of speech from dangerous propaganda. When it comes to fascist or racist material, thinking people may feel able to make the distinction. But on the subject of paedophilia, it is usually the case of the blind leading the blind. The 'Letter from a Paedophile' (*Index* 5/00) is a case in point.

Anyone who sexually abuses a child is a paedophile. Paedophilia is a compulsion and addiction. Prison sentences and treatment programmes are largely ineffective. Many paedophiles are presented as pillars of society – middle-class, well dressed, articulate, charming and engaged in ordinary social pursuits. The writer cites a number of famous paedophiles as if name-dropping supports his case.

Few paedophiles set out to physically hurt or frighten their victims. On the contrary, they go to immense trouble to engage in what is known as 'grooming'. Grooming is done with great stealth and patience – gaining the parent's and child's trust. Children are naturally sensual – not sexual – and before they know it they are in at the deep end and are being told they wanted it or asked for it. So much for your correspondent's assertion that children are in control.

Your correspondent, while setting himself up as the child's best friend, admits his predilection for nine- and ten-year-old girls. They will be dropped when they reach ten and he will move on to his next victim – so much for genuine love of children.

Prisons, mental health institutions, dole queues, divorce courts, doctors' surgeries, alcohol and drug centres, and children's homes are significantly populated by victims of sexual abuse. The price paid by the individual can be lifelong social dysfunction and unhappiness.

There are thousands of paedophiles out there known to communities who appear to be beyond the law all their lives. Your correspondent refers sneeringly to the 'sexual abuse industry'. Sadly this is in disarray due to lack of funding and of skilled and experienced staff, to government policy, inertia and misogyny.

Do paedophiles ever ask themselves why undeveloped children with immature sexual organs would choose to engage in premature sexual activity with a middle-aged man, thus becoming emotionally estranged from non-abusing adults and isolated from their peers? ❏

PM Colledge

news in the

• **Gleb on the Web** President Vladimir Putin's campaign to portray himself as a liberal reformer suffered a glitch when it became clear that his spin-doctor did not quite share the ex-KGB man's sunny view of the media. Gleb Pavlovsky, the man charged with improving Putin's public image, lashes out on his website at those who reduced state censorship during *perestroika*. Pavlovsky concludes by blaming press freedom for the 'degradation and destruction of society'.

• **Famous last words** 'There is not one of you who would dare to write his honest opinion,' John Swainton of the *New York Times* told colleagues at his retirement party in September. 'The business of a journalist is to destroy truth, to lie outright, to pervert, to vilify, fall at the feet of Mammon and sell himself for his daily bread. We are tools, vessels of rich men behind the scenes, we are jumping jacks. They pull the strings; we dance. Our talents, our possibilities and our lives are the properties of these men. We are intellectual prostitutes.' So saying, he sailed away into an honest retirement.

• **Press-Jianged** Jiang Zemin, the meticulously preened president of China, flew into a rage with the Hong Kong media when a reporter asked if Beijing's support for Chief Executive Tung Chee hwa amounted to an 'imperial order' for Tung to be given a second term. Jiang exploded: 'If there is anything wrong with your reporting, you will be held responsible! Got it?' he screeched, switching between Mandarin, Cantonese and English. Tung, who beamed affably throughout, later said Jiang 'merely gave kind encouragement. I think it is a good thing for people to improve their standards.'

• **Kill the pig!** Mothercare, the UK children's clothing chain, reported in mid-November that it had received a horde of requests for child products in Winnie-the-Pooh and Piglet livery to be cruelly censored. The popular characters of AA Milne's children's stories market bath mats, toys, pyjamas and games, but the despised status of the pig in Islam has made many Muslim customers shy away from buying kiddywear. Mothercare lawyers are now looking into the legal implications of partitioning the cuddly twosome and airbrushing out the bacon.

● **Fly bastards** Cut-price airline Ryanair was sued by British Airways in October for trademark infringement and 'disseminating malicious falsehood in advertisements'. The case stemmed from a 1999 Ryanair ad which charged: 'Expensive BA----DS'. On 5 December, the High Court ruled that the advertising campaign was honest and fair, and that no element amounted to 'more than vulgar abuse'.

● **Trainer in mouth** US giant Nike double-faulted the Sydney Olympics when two of its ads were disqualified by the US networks. One, featuring sprinter Suzy Hamilton fleeing in her Nike trainers from a chainsaw-wielding maniac, was condemned as 'stupid', 'repellent', 'disgusting' and 'misogynistic' by women's groups. Unabashed, Nike responded by releasing another which described the disabled as 'drooling misshapen' husks – skilfully timed to coincide with the grand finale of the Paralympic Games.

● **Smear campaign** Food manufacturer Heinz was condemned by the Broadcasting Standards Commission (BSC) on 26 October after a commercial for its salad cream caused viewers to bombard the advertising watchdog with complaints. The ad shows a dirty, bedraggled man reaching into a litterbin to retrieve a half-eaten sandwich which he then proceeds to smear with the product. It ends with the slogan: 'Heinz tastes good with anything.' The BSC found that the commercial 'exceeded acceptable boundaries in its mocking of homeless people'.

● **Cartoon crash** The Turkish broadcasting regulator ordered ATV off the air in early December for broadcasting an episode of the cartoon *Pokémon* in defiance of a government ban. The order was issued after two children injured themselves leaping out of a top-floor window while attempting to imitate characters from the show. Four-year-old Ferhat Altinbas, who sustained a broken leg in the fall, told doctors: 'I am a Pokémon and I flew like one.' Apparently not.

● **Witness for the prosecution** Two Georgian Jehovah's Witnesses, victims of defrocked priest Basili Mkalavishvili's pogrom against their religion, were convicted in October of 'hooliganism'; the mob that attacked them was acquitted. Marian Abaradze and Zaza Koshadze, both of whom were beaten with iron crosses by disciples of 'Father Basili', were sentenced to three years' probation and six months' imprisonment respectively. The attackers walked free, but two elderly women who witnessed the incident in Gldani were successfully brought to Georgian justice.

● **Memory rezoning** A memorial cross in the Mojave Desert, built to commemorate America's war dead, is to be removed because it 'represents an illegal endorsement of religion on public land'. The National Park Service promised in November to dismantle the monument after the American Civil Liberties Union (ACLU) threatened to sue for 'promoting Christian beliefs over others'. The ACLU's Peter Eliasberg opined: 'Federal park land is for all of us, whether we are Jewish, Buddhist, Christian, Muslim or none.' Veteran John Sandleman pointed out: 'Many thousands of men and women died in the wars to protect the civil liberties of Americans. It's sad that we cannot remember them the way we wish.'

● **Demon cake** *Titanic* fever has hit Kabul and the Taliban authorities are having trouble sinking it. Officially, no one should have seen the film – cinema and television were banned in September 1996 – but bootleg copies circulate among those wily enough to conceal their videos from the religious police. Markets are doing a roaring trade with under-the-counter sales of clothes, lipstick and perfume bottles adorned with images of the doomed ship. Barbers offer a Leonardo DiCaprio cut, though the law on 'untrimmed beards' spoils the effect somewhat. With the craze extending to wedding ceremonies, the Taliban decided to put its collective foot down. 'The Chicken Street food stores,' reads an announcement in *Shariat Weekly*, 'should know that moulding their wedding cakes in the shape of the *Titanic* ship and other designs is something against our national and Islamic culture.'

● **Food fatwa** Hungry Italians shouldn't drop into McDonald's because the restaurant chain is 'too Protestant'. Writing in *Avvenire* in November, theologian Massimo Salani attacked the godless eating habits of its old religious adversary and called on Catholics to resist the temptations of the Big Mac. Salani declared that McDonald's encouraged the 'individualistic relationship between man and God established by Martin Luther' and accused its products of 'negating the holiness of food'. Having thus disposed of the Protestant diet, Salani turned his attention to Muslim eating habits. He condemned the Koran's strict regulations and emphasis on fasting as 'unnutritious'.

• **Second time around** Ten years since he was first elected president, the charismatic ex-priest Jean-Bertrand Aristide was returned to power after an election on 26 November boycotted by Haiti's main opposition parties. The Democratic Convergence, a 17-strong coalition of social democrats to supporters of ex-dictator François Duvalier, claimed that the council that organised the poll was controlled by Aristide's Lavalas Family Party.

The dispute began after the May parliamentary elections when an Organisation of American States mission accused the electoral council of using a vote-counting method that clearly favoured a Lavalas Family Senate. Having polled poorly in the first round, the opposition parties seized on the criticism as a reason to withdraw most of their candidates from a second-round run-off.

In the absence of international observers, the issue of voter participation rate was hotly contested. The official tally was 62%, but the Democratic Convergence estimated turnout as low as five per cent. Whatever the reality, analysts agree that Aristide remains by far the most popular politician in Haiti, and that he would have easily won a free and fair election.

Whether he will be able to implement his populist programme of job creation, improved services and partnership between the state and the private sector remains to be seen. Unlike in 1991, when he faced a hostile legislature, this time he will govern with a majority. The army, which overthrew his first administration was disbanded after his forced return to office by a UN invasion in 1994.

But the economy has failed to recover from the international sanctions against the 1991–94 military regime, and future aid is in doubt as the donors question the 2000 election results. Furthermore, many of Aristide's supporters have since turned against what they perceive as his dictatorial tendencies.

Charles Arthur

• **Changing texts** The teaching of history, particularly recent history, is at the centre of a political row that threatens the Italian tradition of freedom of instruction.

On 9 November, Francesco Storace, a member of the Alleanza Nazionale, the party that emerged from the neo-fascist Movimento Sociale Italiano in 1995, voted for the creation of a commission to evaluate textbooks in the region of Lazio, of which he is Council President. According to his motion, many of these books 'falsify or ignore certain pages of Italian history, portraying them in a sectarian way' which 'hinders the reconstruction of a national identity common to all Italians'.

The council is to subsidise authors to 'elaborate' new textbooks for introduction into the public educational system. Reactions to the proposal have included demonstrations by teachers and students, culminating in a parliamentary debate in which President Giuliano Amato reaffirmed the right to freedom of instruction, under article 33 of the constitution.

Secondary teachers have enjoyed remarkable freedom since the foundation of the republic in 1946. The state defines courses, but exercises no control over the books used to teach them. That choice is left to committees of teachers, parents and student representatives. As for content, whether Marxist, Catholic or liberal in accent, all textbooks share the general spirit of anti-fascism which all political parties espouse – except, of course, the neo-fascists.

Currently, Lazio has only the option to write its textbooks, not to impose them, and certainly not to prevent the adoption of any 'unwelcome' alternatives. But a bill currently making its way through parliament is expected to give unprecedented powers to the regions to determine the teaching materials used. Though undefined as yet, they could open the way for political intrusion into the sphere of secondary education.

Luigi Cajani

● **Dissidents honoured** To those who remember Poland's long fight for democracy, from the founding of the Solidarity free trade union in 1980, through the dark days of Martial Law,

to the collapse of the Communist government in August 1989, the name of the London-based fortnightly bulletin *Uncensored Poland* evokes special echoes. For almost 12 years, until it was finally wound up at the end of 1991, it provided a unique window into that country: materials from the underground press, statements by opposition leaders, documents leaked by sympathisers within the ruling apparatus and a day-by-day calendarium of repression, censorship and the endemic abuses of human and civil rights.

It gave in-depth background to events which hit the world headlines, like the murder of the Solidarity priest Father Jerzy Popieluszko, and also chronicled the less eye-catching news – the nerve-wearing petty-minded acts of official persecution and the long haul back to democracy as the regime finally realised that it had lost control. Throughout its existence *Uncensored Poland* had the well-deserved reputation of being a uniquely comprehensive and authoritative source on which journalists and politicians throughout the world could rely for timely and accurate information.

Eleven years after it closed, the London-based team behind *Uncensored Poland* has been honoured for their work: by decree of Polish President Aleksander Kwasniewski, the three principal editors, Antoni Pospieszalski, Krzysztof Pszenicki and Jan Radomyski, have been awarded Commander's Crosses of the Order of the Rebirth of Poland. Two co-workers, Janusz Cywinski and Irma Stypukowska, have received the Knights Cross of that Order.

Vera Rich

● **Double vision** The 7 November screening by South African Broadcasting Corporation (SABC) of a video showing police dogs and their handlers savaging a group of blacks, evoked a battery of protests from viewers, but the South Africa Broadcasting Complaints Commission refused to censure the makers of the investigative news programme *Special Assignment.*

The film, passed anonymously to SABC, showed six white police unloading three Mozambican immigrants from a van on to a piece of wasteland. The men are immediately pummelled and thrown to the ground. Then, in what one of the officers jokingly labels 'a training exercise', four Alsatians are unleashed and proceed to maul them. One of the handlers refers to his dog as a 'kaffir-biter'.

The producers consulted Safety and Security Minister Steve Tshwete before broadcasting the footage. Tshwete's decision to sanction the programme was upheld by the Complaints Commission, which ruled that a channel could legitimately show 'material which is shocking where, to its mind, it serves a legitimate and compelling purpose'.

The SABC's decision to air the video was applauded by Archbishop Desmond Tutu. He said the footage exposed the prevailing racism in state institutions. 'You have to be extraordinary not to succumb to those horrendous forces,' he said. But the viciousness of the incident awakened many to a form of racism increasingly prevalent in South African society – attacks on *makwerekwere*, or immigrants from Zimbabwe, Zambia, Nigeria and Mozambique. More than ten Nigerian foreign workers have been murdered in Hillbrow since 1997.

Raymond Louw, editor of the weekly *Southern Africa Report,* suggests that some whites discriminate between attacks on black South Africans, which they censor as racist, and attacks on illegal black immigrants, which they do not. In a recent editorial, he asked: 'Did the policemen responsible for the dog attack allow themselves to be filmed because they felt that the episode was exempt from the prohibition of old-style racism because the victims were foreign nationals?'

DG

MALACHI O'DOHERTY

Teddy Bear's picnic

**Internecine Republican strife muzzles debate
on the issues that matter**

Anthony McIntyre was not at home the night they came for him. His partner, Carrie, who is pregnant, was at home when Republicans loyal to Gerry Adams picketed their Ballymurphy house a second time. McIntyre is a Republican who is not loyal to Gerry Adams, and that is why it is no longer safe for him to live at home.

The gossip in the district says he is a tout, an informer. The basis of that claim is that he is a writer and a political thinker who embarrasses the Provisional IRA. He has accused them of murdering Joseph O'Connor, a leader of the rival Real IRA, the group that massacred 29 people in the Omagh bombing and continues to wage an armed campaign against the peace process.

McIntyre's own campaign against the Good Friday Agreement has been more elegant and more eloquent. Now that the heavies are inching closer to his own front door, he is beginning to wonder if it has also had more effect. He does not support the Real IRA but nor does he support murder of its members either. 'We think the shooting of O'Connor was a dreadful message to send to the group that carried out the Omagh bombing. It tells them that the use of weapons to settle political disputes still has a legitimacy within the Republican tradition. It also renders null and void the criticism that Sinn Fein made of the Omagh bombing. How can they criticise the Omagh bombing and yet reinforce the intellectual well from which those bombers drink?'

Gerry Adams has himself described Anthony McIntyre as a 'fellow traveller' with the Real IRA. That is the sort of loose talk that could get a man into trouble. In Republican tradition it is called 'felon setting', setting somebody up for arrest or attack. Adams is himself very touchy when he is treated to the same sort of thing.

Joseph O'Connor was shot dead in his car, half a mile from where
Anthony McIntyre lives. The O'Connor family blamed the Provisionals
and McIntyre agreed. He and another member of the Republican
Writers Group, which he helped form, issued a statement to the press,
pointing the finger at them. The Provos were not at all pleased.
McIntyre and his partner had already been in trouble with the IRA for
their outspoken comments and their writing. He is an irritant to the
IRA and the Gerry Adams leadership. He is a also a respected academic
writer, with a PhD on the growth of Sinn Fein. He edits two magazines:
Fourthwrite, a platform for criticism of the Adams peace strategy, calling
Sinn Fein back to core Republican ideology, though not to violence;
and *Other View*, co-edited with the Loyalist Billy Mitchell, and aimed
at presenting debate between Loyalists and Republicans on issues that
divide them.

Carrie Twomey was running a website for the Republican Writers
Group and an alternative Republican bulletin board for discussion on
Republican issues. Two IRA men visited McIntyre and Twomey at
home and complained about the bulletin board. There was a quarrel.
The IRA men left in a sour mood.

A contributor to the board had written a follow-up to claims in
the media in November that a high-ranking informer operated inside
the Provisionals, and had been known to the army by the code name
'Steak Knife'. The contributor, using his own code name, 'Teddy Bear',
speculated on who Steak Knife might have been. He listed ten leading
Republicans who were not in jail when a Loyalist hit squad was
reportedly directed away from Steak Knife.

By the sort of convergence that could deflect you from the heart of
this story, the hit squad that went looking for Steak Knife, not knowing
that he was working for the army, was redirected to another target. It
killed Francisco Notarantonio, and it just happens that he was the
grandfather of Joseph O'Connor.

After the visit from the two IRA men, Carrie Twomey closed down
the website, fearing that she was at risk of being targeted for what others
said on it. Then O'Connor was killed. McIntyre and another member of
the writers' group, Tommy Gorman, published a statement blaming the
Provisionals for the murder. That was when the first picket came.

McIntyre got the measure of it from talking to friends who witnessed
it. 'There was a massive IRA presence on the estate, patrols and cars, 12

Dublin, December 2000: US President Bill Clinton and Hillary Clinton with Gerry Adams.
Credit: Camera Press / Rota

men in one house and six in another. They were shouting things
like: "Are you judge and jury?" They also had placards that attacked
Fourthwrite: "*Fourthwrite* is shite".' He doesn't know if they came to hurt
him: the IRA members could have been with the picket just to frighten
him, to provide the muscle for an attack on him or just to keep order.
'Or maybe I was to get my head kicked in and the next day there would
have been a statement from Gerry Adams expressing regret that the
whole thing had got out of hand.'

Sinn Fein says the community is angry with McIntyre because he
has endangered members whom local gossip blames for the murder of
O'Connor. McIntyre says he has not named the killers in his writing,
just the organisation. He has not called on people to report the killers
to the police; but he has called for a local inquiry. 'The Provisionals say
they didn't kill O'Connor. In that case they should be as concerned as
anyone else about people being murdered in Ballymurphy; they should
not be trying to silence the people who want an inquiry.'

For Twomey and McIntyre and their allies in the Republican
Writers Group, this is a free speech issue. They believe Sinn Fein polices

expression in its own territory. Some of the writers in the Republican Writers Group look back on decades of imprisonment and support for political murder and ask what their own 'bloody investment' was for, if the political result is little different from what was available decades ago in 1973 when the first power-sharing executive was established. They want to see a moral balance between what they exacted for their cause and what they achieved. McIntyre says: 'The Good Friday Agreement is about including Republicans and excluding Republicanism. It has achieved none of the core objectives of Republicanism. It is partitionist, and I have to ask myself, why should we have fought so long and inflicted so much and sustained so much in order to settle for something that Ted Heath offered us.'

Not that he wants to resume the killing. 'If at the end of the day, if the only choices facing Republicans were an armed campaign and the Adams strategy, we have to opt for the Adams strategy because it reduces the chances of leaving bodies on Omagh's streets or Enniskillen's streets. But I don't think the intellectual space has been exhausted and that these are the only alternatives.'

His is not a popular political cause. No party endorses it. Most people in Ireland believe Gerry Adams worked a miracle in bringing the IRA into a settlement that gave them so little of what they had been killing for. The experience of McIntyre and Twomey suggests, however, that Provo muscle and Provo guns are now working in the service of that settlement against any on their patch who would query it. ❏

Malachi O'Doherty is a freelance journalist in Belfast working for the Belfast Telegraph, *the* Scotsman *and the BBC. He is the author of* The Trouble With Guns *(Blackstaff Press)*

ALICE LAGNADO

The silenced war

The world's attention is elsewhere while Chechens suffer at the hands of their own rebels as well as Russian occupying forces

Mrs Koka Uzayeva was sitting in her kitchen in Itum Kale, a town deep in the mountains of southern Chechnya on the Georgian border, making supper for her extended family. She complained of the disappointment she felt in both Russian and Chechen leaders. 'To hell with Maskhadov, Basayev, Putin, Yeltsin. May they all be buried in one grave,' she cried. A moment later, she lost her fire. 'Listen, have you heard when the war will end? Surely it can't go on?' Mrs Uzayeva's plea to a visiting journalist for news of what was happening on her own doorstep is typical of the thousands of civilians left in Chechnya.

President Vladimir Putin trumpets the end of hostilities, but the war is still a harsh reality. Civilians are caught between the twin threats of brutal Russian contract soldiers and rebel leaders with no regard for their own compatriots. During the heavy bombardment in the winter of 1999 and the spring of 2000, the war was given maximum media coverage. Now it is almost invisible, a matter of little concern to the international community, diplomats or journalists.

It is true that the military onslaught has diminished dramatically, but Russian planes bomb the southern mountains on a daily basis and, sometimes, Grozny too. At the same time, Russian troops regularly beat, torture and murder civilians in a network of detention camps. Everyone knows someone who has had violence done to them by the soldiers. 'In some villages almost every family has been affected,' said Marie Struthers, a Human Rights Watch (HRW) researcher who spent two and a half weeks in Ingushetia last November. The latest method of torture is the 'Maskhadov phone call', named after Chechnya's President Aslan Maskhadov. 'Would you like to call Maskhadov?' ask the soldiers, before sending an electrical shock between a prisoner's ears.

*Grozny, 2000: Medent Sultanova, 48, in her
two-room – once three-room – apartment*

Grozny, 2000: children play among the rubble

Detention camps are dotted all over Chechnya and just outside its borders in disused buildings, at military bases and in underground pits from one to 10m deep, holding between two to 50 prisoners. Because the prisoners are blindfolded, no one knows exactly where the camps are. Chechens have also been taken to Russian prisons in Pyatigorsk and Stavropol. Soldiers sometimes go on the rampage through villages, attacking anyone in their path. Last winter civilians reported a new phenomenon: gangs of masked men breaking into homes at night and kidnapping the inhabitants. HRW found 13 such cases in one village, Yermolovskoye.

Fear and powerlessness are the two overriding features of life. There is no work and little food; people are kept prisoner in their homes by the curfew and the checkpoint system prevents free travel for those without a lot of money. A family who recently returned to their bombed house in Itum Kale from a refugee camp in Georgia had to pay nearly US$4,000 to go home.

There is almost no independent, reliable information about the Russian bombing. On a trip to Vedeno in November, locals said they heard the occasional bombing in the distance, but did not know from where. The only news is the few lines on the Russian news agency, Interfax. A typical report reads: 'Helicopters of the ground forces and the Interior Ministry flew over 40 combat missions on Monday.' The information disseminated by the armed forces is, as in any war, insufficient; the Chechen rebel websites, some fanatically anti-western or anti-Semitic, are no more credible.

The government continues to stage whistle-stop tours for journalists but hardly anyone goes because of the lack of demand from editors; in any case, the trips reveal so little. The government claims concern for our safety, but no soldiers ever examined my papers though I crossed numerous checkpoints. Chechens say anyone, including fighters, can bribe their way through.

This war is longer and more bloody than the conflict in Kosovo, but it commands less attention, less aid and less foreign intervention. There are only around 30 aid agencies on the ground, partly because aid workers in the past have been kidnapped or killed, but the authorities also make it difficult to operate and no agency can work in the south. Unlike the Kosovars, most of whom returned home after a few months,

Pervomaiskoe, Vedeno district, outside Grozny, 2000: Raibek, pro-Moscow deputy head of the Vedeno administration, with his son Salambek

the 170,000 displaced Chechens have languished in camps across the border in Ingushetia for over a year.

Any reporter who visits comes across stories of human rights abuse. I wrote the first in a British newspaper about the torture camps in November 1999, the beginning of a tide of tales of attacks on Chechens by out-of-control soldiers. On my last six-day trip one year later, I saw how the terror was continuing. We arrived in Itum Kaleb a few days after 60 soldiers from GRU, the military intelligence arm, had rampaged through the village, watched wordlessly by the hundreds of police from Novosibirsk stationed there.

The army-appointed head of the village, who stopped them beating two Chechen police officers half to death, was 'a white crow', as the Russians say, someone very unusual. His biggest problem, he said, was the soldiers who came to Chechnya to 'throw their weight around'. What he needed, he said, was men to maintain law and order and rebuild the destroyed villages. Unusually, he reported the incident to the Ministry of Defence for investigation, and talked on record to a journalist.

In Vedeno, Raibek – the pro-Moscow Chechen who heads the district – alleged that Rizvan Imaliyev, a 20-year-old economics student, was killed by a gang of men in military fatigues. Villagers said he was shot at close range. The case is not as solid as the one in Itum Kale, but it was a sign that the killing has not stopped. Shamil Basayev and Khattab, the two most prominent guerrilla leaders, are known to live in the Vedeno district, untouched by the military, while many lesser commanders live quietly in Moscow. The Kremlin's claim that it is fighting to catch and punish these men sounds hollow.

Civilians are also tormented by the rebels. During the first Chechen war in 1994–96, a certain amount of hope attached to these men: now they are despised. Many are hoodlums who have carried out extensive kidnappings and torture of Chechens, Russians and foreigners. They are markedly different from the ordinary men who fought to defend their homes. In November 1999, a group of rebels fired at villagers in Gekhi, 20km south-west of Grozny, wounding at least five. One man told HRW how armed fighters had started shooting at him and three others at a checkpoint when they asked the rebels not to enter the village for fear of Russian reprisals.

'They started to shoot, at very close range, aiming straight at our legs,' he said. Another man added: 'We provoked them in no way. They wanted to get into our village to attack the Russian positions. But we don't have rebel fighters here, and we don't want them.' In December, during Ramadan, rebels reportedly set off a car bomb near a mosque in Alkhan Yurt killing 21 people, many of them children.

Ordinary Chechens do not like the rebels, but they are forced to tolerate them. The under-reporting of abuse by guerrilla commanders tends to strengthen the Russian hand. They say western journalists are biased, wilfully ignoring the record of some commanders who, before the war,

*Grozny, 2000: Vyacheslav Baklashov, invalided, at the ruined home
for aged people in which he lived with his wife before the war*

were uneducated martial arts enthusiasts, involved in crime, with little
or no interest in building a democratic society. How would we have
dealt with a region where kidnapping had become the only functioning
industry, they ask? The standard response to criticism of excessive
behaviour by Russian troops is to show a film of Chechen kidnappers
cutting captives' fingers off, and then beheading them. It is an extreme
and distasteful reaction, but they may have a point. ❏

Alice Lagnado is a correspondent for The Times *in Moscow. All photographs
are by Yuri Kozyrev*

DAÏKHA DRIDI

God only knows

Algerians are suffering a paralysis of conscience brought on by the 1999 amnesty that has brought the killers back into the community

From time to time, Ali Merabet knocks on the door of one of the press offices in Algiers. He has a grim smile, and is clutching an attaché case stuffed with papers that bear witness to his tireless shuttling between courts and police stations. When I met him for the first time last year, he was wandering around the Mitidja plain, 20 minutes away from Algiers, in Raïs, close to the killing fields of Bentalha (*Index* 6/1997).

Merabet was on hunger strike while carrying out an investigation near a field which, he claims, contains the mass grave where his two brothers are buried. After 13 days the judiciary ordered the excavations to begin. A year later, Merabet is still doing the rounds. Today he's preparing a national campaign to press for the mass graves to be finally opened, but the press takes little interest in a story that, after all, has become fairly commonplace here.

His two brothers were abducted, tortured and murdered by members of an Islamist group. He founded an association for the families of victims of terrorist abductions; there are almost 5,000 families in the same plight, unable to understand why the judicial system fails to search the places where their family members may be buried. Several mass graves have been opened since 1996, and the contents widely reported. But, for the most part, the press never asked questions about the procedure for identifying the bodies, even though they were exhumed in the full glare of publicity. What happened to the unearthed remains has not been disclosed, and not one of the families of kidnapped relatives has been approached to assist with identification.

Every Wednesday, people driving along one of the smartest of Algiers' main roads look away in embarrassment, trying not to see that

Algiers, 7 May 2000: a woman holds a picture of her missing son, in a demonstration by 300 mothers outside the Algerian Ministry of Justice. Credit: Popperfoto

the women shouting 'give us back our children!' outside the human rights office are still there, clutching photos of their dead. They are fewer since the first public demonstration was permitted in June 1998, but they never miss a Wednesday. They don't know if their children are in one of the mass graves, or still alive. All they know is that they were kidnapped at night and have disappeared without trace. They don't bother the newspapers any more, because everyone has had enough of their stories because they're all alike.

The national association for families of kidnap victims lists nearly 7,000 cases of persons abducted by the security services. Little Meriem, for example, is the daughter of a journalist. He was kidnapped while she was still a baby; she's growing up very fast and has behavioural problems. Her mother, Safia, can no longer cope with questions like: 'Tell me about Daddy,' or 'Why do the other kids at school have a daddy?' Five years after her husband was taken away, Safia still does not know whether or not to say to her daughter: 'Forget your father, he's dead.' She's giving it a bit longer.

'Truth and Justice' was the slogan used by the victims' families' organisations at their demonstrations after the Civil Concord Act was passed by parliament on 13 July 1999, a few months after Abdelaziz Bouteflika became president. Following the series of major massacres in Algeria in 1997–98, the act laid down a programme to remove or reduce any legal sanctions against members of armed groups, provided they gave themselves up within six months. The law excluded those who had committed any crime during the course of the seven-year insurrection. The majority of Algerians thought that the question in the related referendum, 'Do you agree with President Bouteflika's proposal for restoring peace?' meant the government intended to put a stop to the bombings and killings. They were prepared to agree, if the terror came to an end.

Ever since the period of grace ended on 13 January 2000, poor districts in the major towns and villages in the hinterland have been rife with stories about the 'return of the killers'. Families are recognising the people who killed their relatives. People are beginning to waver. What do they mean by giving a free pardon to known murderers? Why is it that the state which was relentless, prepared even to use illegal methods when it came to subduing Islamist groups, is now so ready to act as if nothing had happened? Many hide their hatred behind a wall of silence. A few have decided to act, like the 17-year-old who shot at close range his father's murderer, a member of the AIS, the armed wing of the FIS (Islamic Salvation Front). He is now in prison in the eastern town of Jijel.

A year ago, I went to meet a reformed member of the GIA (Armed Islamic Group) in the same part of the country. I wanted to understand why these people had made war not only against the state, but against people, and to find out the reasons for his surrender. Like other repentant terrorists I spoke to, he replied in a guarded fashion. But he was one of the few to give an offhand answer when asked whether he had ever killed anyone: 'God only knows.' Algerians say: 'God and military intelligence know.' It is difficult not to see, behind this spectacular turnaround in the state's relations with the armed groups, some sort of secret deal intended to whitewash both sides. If no one bothers the Islamic groups about the crimes they committed over a seven-year period, no one will look too closely into the legacy of torture, summary execution and abduction committed by the state. To put the GIA or AIS murderers on trial would give the republic's torturers something to worry about.

Today, a year and a half after the Civil Concord Act officially called on all victims of violence to keep quiet, there are no more demonstrations. Fewer and fewer people now call for the implicit amnesty for terrorists and the security personnel to be revoked. But the war is still going on, far away from Algiers and the major towns. They are carefully sheltered from the negative impact of any acts of violence which reflect badly on the new face of Algeria which the Bouteflika government is trying to depict. Algiers is pretending to forget. People don't talk about the 'little massacres' which happen every day. Livestock farmers, young soldiers, whole families in isolated houses in the countryside are still hacked to death, but they are ignored except by the privately owned press.

In an attempt to break this silence – at his own personal level at least – Noureddine spends a lot of time in discussion groups and chat rooms which Algerian cybernauts use to talk about 'the war and the poor people who are still dying'. Usually all he gets are insults, but his contributions are humane and full of humour. It's his way of showing solidarity with people that no one wants to know about. But the dead are no good for the kind of business frenzy that has resulted from the recent opening up of the economy. Everyone wants to do deals quickly 'before the Algerian ship sinks once and for all'. It is as if, since they have miraculously survived the horrors of the war, Algerians today have one goal only: to survive the horrors of a social context transformed by the structural adjustment programme.

Worn-out and shell-shocked, Algerians leaf through daily reports of suicides; police officers killing themselves after killing their families, adolescents hanging themselves, old people poisoning themselves with acid. Everyone takes refuge in their personal history, putting up shutters against an outside world which offers nothing but more aggression. The Civil Concord Act has not kept its word: Algerians have not spoken out about what happened to them. They are shut away, concealing layers of mute suffering in an ailing collective memory, strictly controlled by those in power. Ali Merabet, Safia Fahassi and her little Meriem, the mothers of thousands of soldiers killed in appalling conditions, or of the thousands of citizens brutally tortured or coldly executed: all these phantoms no one wants to see. Even the slaughter in Palestine – once a sacred cause for Algerians – failed to get a response, though it shook the rest of the Arab world.

Silent though it may be, the Algerian collective memory can still be cruel. At the moment, it is being asked to remember because of a debate about French responsibility for the large-scale torture practised by the colonial army during the war of liberation. This may be a matter between Frenchman and Frenchman, but it is interesting because of the obstinate indifference with which it is treated in Algeria. Why? Because it's about amnesties, war crimes and about a word seen as terrible by Algerian consciences: torture. These feelings are connected to the relationship between a nation and its past sufferings; but they are once again part of the present. Today's Algerians may not find French qualms of conscience very interesting because they remind them of their own responsibility for the horrifying picture of all that lies inside their frontiers that has gone unpunished. ❏

Daïkha Dridi *is a reporter for* Quotidien d'Oran. *Translated by Mike Routledge*

FELIPÉ FERNANDEZ-ARMESTO

Writing – and rewriting – the Millennium

The contemporary pursuit of the Millennium has returned millenarianism from the wilder fringes of apocalyptic prophecy to the historical mainstream: it has become ordinary, respectable even. But in the interests of a quiet life and good government – democracy, let's say – we should hope to hear a little less of it in coming years

As the year 2000 drew to a close, most predictions failed to come true. While pundits came out to watch, Millenarians stayed at home. Those hoping for cosmic fireworks got only damp squibs: the 'Millennium Bug' stayed in its burrow; the only panic was a bit of panic-buying.

In the historiography of Millenarianism, however, the turn of the Millennium really does seem to mark a modest turning point. Three effects are discernible. First, Millenarianism has been rehabilitated as respectable; second, it has been flattered as important; finally, historians' work has contributed to Millennium-weariness. In the new century we can hope for a spell – probably only a short one – of revulsion from apocalyptic gloom and glee. If this happens, it will be a valuable achievement: eschatological prophecy has a long history of political abuse, usually in the service of authoritarian and totalitarian agendas.

Of course, it was never rational to expect much Millenarianism to be triggered by the flick of the calendar. People are silly enough to expect or demand change at the turn of decades or centuries and the emotions they invest sometimes generate the force of self-fulfilling prophecies.

Predictions of the end of the world, however, have rarely coincided with such moods. The year 2000 marks a thousand years since nothing-in-particular. It is quite close to the two-thousandth anniversary of the incarnation of Christ but – owing to an error of computation by the monk who devised the system – misses it by a few years. Even among Millenarian Christians, the incarnation has only occasionally figured as a key date from which to calculate the end of the world. Most movements have expected Armageddon in years not divisible, in our system of reckoning, by 1,000 or even 100. The year 1260 was the one that aroused most apocalyptic excitement in the Middle Ages in Europe. Various prophets staked their reputations on dates in the 1670s. The early Adventists experienced their Great Disappointment in 1844. In the 1990s, the pet numerologist of the Nation of Islam predicted The End in 2001. David Koresh expected the world to last until 2007. Adherents of the 'Maya Prophecies' focused on 2012. 'Aquarians' backed a vague period of transition to the New Age: this is a sensible strategy, compared with predictions tied to particular years, as it is hard to falsify. All but the farthest-out of chiliastic loonies know that the way we count years is arbitrary and the likelihood of cosmic shakedown does not increase with the number of noughts.

Nevertheless, to academic scrutineers of chiliasm, the calendar was a magnet. Scholars who turned to the historical study of Millenarianism as 2000 approached were, in some respects, following the news media. Scare stories proliferated about sects and cults that were urging on apocalypse. It is impossible to know whether this is because millennial fervour was genuinely on the increase or because journalists' eyes were trained on the Millennium in search of juicy copy. Well-publicised cases of lethally mad Millenarianism included, in 1993, the tale of the self-appointed 'sinful messiah', David Koresh, who was immolated with 80 followers in Waco. Between 1994 and 1997, almost as many members of the chalet-chic Solar Temple cult perished in mass murders and suicides, ostensibly 'to escape a fate of destruction now awaiting the whole wicked world'. In 1995, followers of a supposedly Buddhist cult leader in Japan tried to stir up collective nirvana with a poison-gas attack on Tokyo's deepest subway station. In March 1997, the bizarre suicide pact known as 'Heaven's Gate' – 39 sad, ageing, 'zoned-out' computer freaks in a villa in California – poisoned themselves in anticipation of the end. They had every New Age trait except optimism. Wrapped up in a nerdish world of web-surfing, they thought – according to their own 'exit videos' – that a UFO would transport them in the trail of a comet before Heaven's gate closed. They posted a red alert on the Internet, warning: 'Planet About To Be Recycled'. The leader's rambling last message emphasised the Millennium's end as the cut-off point for intending fugitives.

The effect of these cases might have been to confirm long-standing prejudices: that Millenarians are weirdos, exiled to the fringe by their own idiocies and incapable of affecting mainstream history. What really happened was the opposite. Dedicated scholars, like Richard Landes, Eugen Weber, Sylvia Thrupp and Frank Graziano, gradually uncovered the history of what might be called 'mainstream Millenarianism'. Landes, for instance, convinced medievalists that it was wrong to suppose that the year 1000 had been unaffected by seriously intended millennial prophecies. Weber traced 'Millenarian' influences on the high politics and big-time religions of the western world from the period of the Roman Empire onwards. Into Latin America's catalogue of mad conquistadors, febrile Franciscans, messianic impostors, nativist rebels and Inca revenants, Frank Graziano threaded the story of how millennial rhetoric and imagery have shaped and seized revolutions and regimes. In this new fabric of Latin American history almost everything since the arrival of Columbus seems to be stitched. Movements as mainstream as the conquest and 'spiritual conquest', the Jesuit enterprise in the *reducciones*, the independence campaigns, modern land reforms and Liberation Theology turn out to be inexplicable or, at least, imperfectly intelligible, except in a millennial context. Bolívar, Sandino, Perón, even Castro and Galtieri, join Quetzalcoatl and Jim Jones in a litany of messianism.

Part of the result has been to make Millenarianism seem ordinary and therefore unthreatening. Millenarianism ought to be respectable: plenty of decent religions with clever, gentle, believers started as 'end-is-nigh' cults, including Mormonism, Adventism and good old Christianity. When I got to know some Mormon historians who were attending a conference of their kind at my college in Oxford, I was surprised to find that such admirably rational people were prepared to profess what seemed to me the obvious nonsense of Mormonism: the angelic revelation to Joseph Smith, the lost tablets of gold, Christ's sojourn in America, the self-consciousness of 'latter-day saints'. They replied that

William Blake, The Vision of the Last Judgement, *1808. Credit: Bridgeman Art Library*

these claims were tainted by their novelty. Give them 2,000 years, they said, and they will seem quaint, at worst – certainly no sillier than the tenets of other Christian sects. Millenarianism matures gracefully. Yet when we meet modern Millenarians we regard them as mad and suspect them as dangerous. Their beliefs are not much more irrational than our fears. More murders, suicides and acts of terrorism happen outside Millenarian circles than within them. So what are we really afraid of?

The scholarship which made Millenarianism seem acceptable also exposed its vulnerability to abuse. Like most forms of violent radicalism, millennial movements usually start among the poor and powerless, who have nothing to lose from a quasi-apocalyptic transformation of the world; but they may grow to threaten peace, take power, generate influence or transmute, as early Christianity did, from a marginal cult into a major force. Millenarianism's is a history of success – not just, as we used to think, of perseverance in failure. Frequently, the effects of its transformations are malign: it has helped to confer power not only on religious charlatans, but also on secular political movements of repellent viciousness. Thanks to the scholarship of Norman Cohn, everyone now knows how indebted the Nazis and Bolsheviks were to the traditions of eschatological prophecy. The Thousand-Year Reich and the Dictatorship of the Proletariat were heirs to the 'Age of the Spirit' predicted by Joachim of Fiore centuries before. In the recent history of Latin America, odious Protestant groups on the extreme right have been willing to collaborate in the destruction of cultures and the exaltation of dictators in their anxiety to prepare the Third World for the Second Coming. Susceptible Catholics were duped and frightened by phoney visionaries. In Guatemala, the regime of General Efraín Rios Montt, self-styled 'King of the New Testament', claimed to be 'driven by the Holy Spirit' in organising the massacre of Indians. At the opposite extreme, the propaganda of Sendero Luminoso promises a 'Millennium beginning' to 'the sound of trumpets, levelling iniquity, making the future be born'. The Internet today is alive with anti-Semitism, cunningly masked as New Age babble. Pseudo-churches advertise ringside seats for the 'death throes of civilisation'. Aum Shinrikyo look-a-likes dream of precipitating the end with spectacular feats of chemical and biological terrorism.

We can expect that Millenarianism – like everything else supposedly scheduled for obliteration – will survive the year 2000. People who find change unbearable expect it to become uncontainable. New kinds of Millenarianism are always emerging. Today's favourites include eco-apocalypticism, asteroid-anticipation, doom-fraught oracles of demographic meltdown or North–South Armageddon. Warnings are audible about the cosmic threat posed by genetic manipulators, the cybercrats of information technology or the corporate monsters of global capitalism. A lot can happen while we are waiting for entropy. We might blow ourselves up or destroy our habitats. We might get replaced by evolution or survive in savagery – for the history of civilisations is a path picked across ruins. There is nothing irrational or improbable about expecting The Apocalypse. The perversity of hoping for it seems pardonable if you take a dispassionately critical view of mankind's achievements so far. But we have had so much of it lately that readers are bored with it and scholarship satiated. As journalists and academics look elsewhere, the lure of Millenarianism will slacken for movements in need of publicity. There is no hope of a future without Millenarianism – that would itself be the realisation of a millennial dream; but at least we can hope, for a time, to hear less about it. ❑

Felipé Fernandez-Armesto's latest book is Civilisations *(Macmillan). He is the author of* Millennium, *and teaches history at Oxford and Queen Mary and Westfield College, London*

Memory and forgetting

History is a tale told by victors. Until the world turns and another version of the truth takes its place: old memories are stirred, forgotten histories see the light of day, a new generation tells a different tale and the past becomes a battleground of competing histories

USSR 1941: a Belarusan orphan returns to his shattered home.
Credit: Slava Katamidze Collection / Hulton Getty Images

STANLEY COHEN

Memory wars and peace commissions

'The truth, the whole truth and nothing but the truth.' The phrase
still resonates in the real world of criminal trials, where victims
and some offenders suffer, and the mythological world of courtroom
dramas, where everyone is paid or entertained. These worlds may
overlap into media events like the OJ Simpson case. The legal version
of truth then loses its symbolic grandeur and moral imperative. Even
in – especially in – the most mundane cases, legal truths are negotiated,
contested and plea-bargained. They cannot be read as historical
records of what happened, let alone why it happened. The image of an
'historical verdict' on the truth retains its potency, but is compromised
by the casual acceptance that there are truths, not 'the truth', and that
legal truths – the 'finding' of not guilty, guilty 'as proven', or wrongful
conviction – are partial and misleading.

Such elementary problems aside, even a complete mosaic of
legal truths cannot create a full or shared knowledge of 'what really
happened'. This is even more obvious when political rather than
personal conflicts are turned into legal events and when the subject is
the *past,* rather than the present. The moral stakes are now much higher:
no less than the 'judgement of history'; the empirical contest is more
open: history can be 'rewritten', revised or even completely denied.

Recent interest in these subjects comes from two sources. One is the
political interest in 'justice in transition': how societies going through
democratic changes deal with atrocities (genocide, political massacres,
torture) committed by the previous regime. The other is the theoretical
interest in concepts such as 'collective memory'. Can a whole society

'remember' or 'forget' its past in the same way as individuals do their autobiographical past? Why are private memories of public events – a coup, a war, an assassination – different from authorised versions? When does an event pass from living memory into history or 'pre-history'? When is collective memory gradually constructed as a shared, democratic experience; when does it result from state-organised 'memory work': memorial sites, ceremonies, marches and monuments?

Heavy demands are made on transitional governments by past victims, local revisionist historians or cosmopolitan human rights advocates. They do want something like the 'whole truth'. But the normal institutions of truth telling have an impossible task. They have to overcome official denials and cover-ups (it didn't happen) and individual denial (I wasn't even there) or amnesia (I must have been there, but I can't remember anything). Then they must convert an already deeply compromised surface history into current testimonies of individual moral responsibility. As if this were not enough, the new society is instructed to take on the utterly obscure task of 'coming to terms' with its the past.

The emerging political discourse about memory is highly dependent on metaphors from personal life. This was most explicit in Germany, where denazification after the end of the Reich and decommunisation after unification were described in the Freudian language of 'working through', 'reckoning with' or 'overcoming' the past. These terms also have connotations of treatment and catharsis. Cultural repression – tacit, unspoken agreements about which pasts are best not talked about – is viewed as analogous to personal repression: how the mind 'forgets' awkward truths, traumatic memories and inadmissible desires. These secular ideas are closely related to religious models of truth-telling and confessional which, for Archbishop Tutu, take on the religious meaning of 'the healing power of the truth'.

But therapists don't usually have to worry about justice or the political implications of telling the truth. In the world of atrocities and human rights, truth-telling is intimately connected with justice, accountability and punishment – whether looking backwards (retribution) or forwards (deterrence). This tense connection is further complicated by the aims of reconciliation and social reconstruction.

This is where we return to the judicial model. No one has seriously refuted Hannah Arendt's conclusion from observing the Eichmann trial: the criminal law is not well suited to control or understand 'administrative massacres'. From the Nuremberg Trials 50 years ago to the current International Criminal Tribunals for Rwanda and the former Yugoslavia and to the International Criminal Court of the future, the issues are the same.

The debate has been dominated by the question of whether collective truth-telling must always lead to judicial accountability because individual moral responsibility is essential to this truth. We investigate the past, that is, in order to identify those responsible and bring them to legal account. In practice, this seldom happens: Pinochet-type amnesties are granted, investigations drag on endlessly and there is the risk that prosecutions would jeopardise fragile democratic gains.

But there is an opposite question about criminal trials. Not whether truths about the past must lead to legal accountability, but whether the criminal law is at all helpful in uncovering these truths. Are the rituals of accusation, proof, attribution of blame and punishment necessary to convert private knowledge to public acknowledgement? This has always been the function of political trials, whether the explicitly staged Stalinist show trials or the other famous boundary-setting trials of history: Jesus, Socrates, Dreyfus, Sacco and Vanzetti, the Rosenbergs, Nuremberg, Eichmann.

The trials of recent political transitions have raised familiar problems:

- **Time**. How far back should we go? For a military junta that lasted for five years after seizing power from a previous democracy, this is less of a problem. But for South Africa, the post-communist societies or the Israeli-Palestinian conflict there is no original sin, no consensual year zero, from which to start accountability for atrocities.

- **Authority and obedience**. Who gave what orders to whom and who obeyed? The essence of administrative atrocities is that these questions are deliberately opaque. Faced with the traditional problems of individual moral responsibility, ambiguous orders, blurred and multiple-command structures, neither judicial justice nor narrative truth are easily served.

- **Degrees of involvement**. How do we identify the different modes of involvement in keeping the old regime going? Occupied Europe is the standard historical precedent: the difference between commission and collusion, between active and passive collusion, between deliberate silence and wilful ignorance (turning a blind eye), the morally repellent but historically accurate idea of collective responsibility. The range runs from the military elite running a Latin American junta to the nuances of involvement, collusion and silence that characterised – in different ways – South Africa and the former communist regimes. There was a distinction in South Africa between police officers carrying out a death-squad execution and low-level government clerks signing a 'pass' which restricted blacks' freedom of movement. But the territory in between is not at all clear.

These three forms of 'drawing the line' – past history, biography and moral geography – pose obvious problems in using criminal law to arrive at the truth. In his recent book *Mass Atrocity, Collective Memory and the Law*, Marc Osiel reviews further problems. Rights of defendants may be sacrificed for the sake of social solidarity. Historical perspective may be lost. Citing faulty precedents or false analogies between past and future controversies may foster delusions of purity and grandeur. Admissions of guilt and repentance required may be too extensive: more people are

Chechen cemetery, 2000: landscape of memory. Credit: Yuri Kozyrev

required to admit more responsibility and to break too strongly with the past. Legal blueprints are ill-suited to evoke and construct a consensual collective memory. Even if the law can deliberately construct collective memory, this may be done dishonestly (by concealing the deliberate formality from the public).

The 1997–98 trial of Maurice Papon well illustrates the problems of legal excavation. Papon, a high-ranking former civil servant (ex-prefect of the Paris police, ex-cabinet minister, close to Mitterand) was sentenced to ten years for complicity in crimes against humanity. After 1940, he helped organise the deportation of 1,500 Jews (about half the city's total) from Bordeaux to Drancy concentration camp near Paris for shipment to the gas chambers. The trial was intimately connected to the entire post-war denial of French collaboration. The myths of mass resistance were challenged after 1968. Since then, France had gone through phases of intense self-scrutiny about its textbook memories of occupation, collaboration and resistance. The trial could hardly produce a consensual version of this contested past. It raised further questions: to be proved guilty, was it enough that Papon had to understand the purpose of the deportations, but not 'agree with it ideologically'? Did he enquire further or was he informed about the fate of the deportees once they were taken off French soil? Why had the prosecution loaded all the guilt on one man, only a middle official in Bordeaux at the time?

The trial revealed neither Papon's moral character nor whether the (young) jurors were more in tune with the new historiography (which acknowledges the choice of Vichy officials in collaborating) or stuck in the old reading: reluctant bending to Nazi coercion to shield their fellow French citizens from something worse. By trying to serve simultaneously justice, history, pedagogy and commemoration, the trial ended up by serving none.

The doubts that Nuremberg raised about justice and truth remain, but matter less today simply because there are so many alternative ways of getting at the truth. Tough investigative journalists are writing the 'history of the present'. They construct instant memories of events – in Bosnia, Rwanda, Kosovo and Gaza – that governments shroud in instant deniability even as they happen. The public denial of past atrocities, notably the Holocaust and other genocides, has been criminalised in many countries. High-profile trials, such as David Irving's libel case, have opened the troublesome connections between present personal world-views and historical narratives. There is also a special obsessive interest – fuelled by identity politics and multiculturalism – in transforming vaguely shared cultural histories into concrete personal experiences. People surf the Internet or travel to different countries to proclaim their pride or confirm their collective martyrdom.

The oldest way to return to past suffering is by commemorating the victims: statues built, streets and city squares named, poetry and prayer, vigils and marches. For many reasons – transitions from repressive regimes, the empowerment of marginal and forgotten minorities, political pressures to remember – there has been an exponential increase in the structures and rituals of commemoration.

James Young's study of the iconography of monuments examines how we remember the past, for what reasons, to what ends and in whose name. His images – as a 'memory tourist' himself – of the European 'landscape of memory', are unforgettable. So are the images in the US Holocaust Museum in Washington DC. The museum tries to create a living memorial. Interactive technology and the personalisation of history allow visitors entering the museum to punch into a computer, receive an identity card for an actual person of the same age and gender who lived in the period, then learn whether the 'twin' survives or perishes.

These and similar populist methods attract much fashionable criticism about exploitation, sentimentality, simplification, dumbing-down, kitsch, pornography, Spielberg-clones, products of the Holocaust industry, Disneyland theme parks, death-camp chic, etc. Some of this condemnation is too glib and elitist: the usual whining of moral and intellectual entrepreneurs who believe they own the past and only they can understand its complexity.

All over the world, commemorations of atrocities have turned into memory wars. With each political oscillation, statues are pulled down, street names changed and public holidays abolished. Some unkempt graveyards in remote villages in Lithuania and Latvia have passed through three identities. Before the collapse of communism, a small hand-painted sign marked the 'Victims of Fascism' who lay in the unmarked graves; the fact that nearly all the dead were Jews from the village was not mentioned at all. In the first wave of re-remembering, signs were changed to identify 'Jewish Victims'. The reascendance of nationalism then gave semiotic priority to 'Lithuanian Victims', all brave fighters against the Nazis and the Stalinists.

As long as there is no literal denial of the historical record of any group's suffering, these disputes about interpretation could make a useful education. As Young suggests, we should not just commemorate but do 'memory-work', not just build monuments, but argue about them, change them and reinterpret them. This is also Osiel's conclusion about the classic political trial: despite its defects as a source of shared memory, the liberal model of a criminal trial – at its best – provides a generous arena for contesting the truth about the past. This can happen even without a trial. As the Pinochet case showed, the simple opening move of the legal game did more to undermine collective amnesia about the Chilean junta that any number of histories or human rights reports.

In April 1977, the Madres de Plaza de Mayo (the Mothers of the Disappeared) began their first silent procession in the Plaza de Mayo, the main square of Buenos Aires. They demanded to know the exact fate of their loved ones, 'disappeared' by the junta during Argentina's Dirty War in 1976–83. Twenty-three years later, they are still walking round the square, joined by the Grandmothers and now the Children of the Plaza de Mayo. Right from the beginning of the junta rule, they grasped just the right way to confront the instant historical denial intended by the term 'disappearance'. They named the names and held up photos, thus rendering personal and knowable what the authorities could not allow. But by carrying their message in a public square, the most open space in the city, they shifted clandestine practices and personal fears into a forbidden realm.

Under a regime so intensely ideological, this was not a 'simple' breaking of silence, a retrieval and reconstruction of a destroyed memory. As Taussig notes, assassinating and disappearing people, then denying this and enshrouding it in clouds of confusion, does not aim to destroy memory, but to relocate collective memory elsewhere. The State's interest was to keep alive memories of brutal repression, but to eliminate them from the public sphere (that is, never to acknowledge the truth officially) and deflect them into personal and family memories. There, in the quiet of domesticity, the fear and nightmares are supposed to remain, stifling any opposition. This is what the Mothers still challenge; as Taussig suggests, they allow the moral and magic powers of the unquiet dead to flow into the public sphere.

The powerful iconography of these women silently pacing around the square draws on Greek tragedy. It has not, until now, been copied elsewhere (see p27). A more modern and empowering image of how to deal with past horrors is the Truth Commision. In various permutations – coupled with justice, coupled with reconciliation or staying 'only' with truth – the model has been reproduced in many countries and justifiably captured universal imagination. The South African Truth and Reconciliation Commission (TRC) under Archbishop Tutu's direction has become the archetype.

The TRC's report is a rare and great affirmation of the quest for truth as a moral value in itself. In building the 'historic bridge' to the new society, the Commission saw its role as establishing as 'complete a picture as possible' of the injustices committed in the past, coupled with a public, official acknowledgement of the untold suffering that resulted from these injustices. 'Untold' means vast, but it also literally means 'untold'. The public hearings, and the intense media coverage, offered a stage for people to tell stories that had never been told.

The Commission knew that it had to arrive at a version of the past that would achieve some common consent: 'We believe we have provided enough of the truth about our past for there to be a consensus about it.' But whose truth? At this point, the report switches to a version of truth-telling far more complicated than the notion of 'consensual truth'. The 'life of the Commission' revealed four notions of truth: factual or forensic; personal or narrative; social or 'dialogue'; healing and restorative.

• **Factual or Forensic Truth**: legal or scientific information that is factual, accurate and objective and is obtained by impartial procedures. At the individual level this means information about particular events and specific people: what exactly happened to whom, where, when and how. At the societal level, this means recording the context, causes and patterns of violations. This requires an interpretation of facts that would at least erode any denials about the past. Disinformation that was once accepted as truth now loses its credibility.

• **Personal or Narrative Truth**: the stories told by perpetrators and, more extensively, victims. This is an opportunity for the healing potential of testimony, for adding to the collective truth and for building reconciliation by validating the subjective experience of people who had previously been silenced or voiceless.

• **Social or Dialogue Truth**: the truth generated by interaction, discussion and debate. The hearings provided transparency and encouraged participation. Conflicting views about the past can be considered and compared. The process matters rather than the end result.

• **Healing and Restorative Truth**: the narratives that face the past in order to go forward. Truth as a factual record is not enough: interpretation must be directed towards goals of self-healing, reconciliation and reparation. This requires the acknowledgement that everyone's suffering was real and worthy of attention.

The report obsessively repeats its driving metaphors of scars and wounds, opening and healing. The past left 'indelible scars' on the collective consciousness; these scars often concealed 'festering wounds'; these wounds must be 'opened up' for the 'cleansing and eventual healing' of the body politic; but it was not enough to open these wounds and then 'sit back for the light of exposure to do the cleansing'.

There will be more wreath-laying ceremonies, museums and memorials; more secret files and destroyed villages revealed; history textbooks rewritten and revised; public inquiries and truth commissions established about all sorts of unresolved conflicts, grievances and disputed facts. But these dual projects – creating a shared memory by delving further into the past and constructing the present in order to ensure a future consensus about the past – are full of unresolvable problems.

First: the tension between the absolute truth required by the ideals of legality, justice and personal moral responsibility, versus today's relativist narratives, the notion that there is neither a single truth nor a sharable memory. Second: the tension between truth-telling as an absolute value, versus the demands of political expediency and pragmatic social policy. Third: drawing the boundaries beyond which a 'consensual' collective memory is not necessary and some contestation is healthy. Fourth: the concept of 'collective memory' itself, especially the tangled links between the psychic and political levels.

A final problem is more paradoxical. The great success of legal and human rights talk may erase the concrete and pictorial sensations on which memory depends. Instead of remembering genocidal killings by what happened, we merely register the debate about whether these events fit the definition of genocide in the United Nations convention. ❏

Stanley Cohen *is professor of sociology at the London School of Economics. This article is based on Chapter 9 of his new book,* States of Denial *(Polity Press, December 2000)*

AVI SHLAIM

Peace confounded

The signing of the Declaration of Principles on Palestinian Self-Government, on 13 September 1993 at the White House, marked the end of one chapter in the history of the Palestinians and the beginning of another. But while the PLO kept its side of the bargain, Israel did not

By signing the agreement negotiated at Oslo by the PLO, and shaking hands with Itzhak Rabin, PLO chairman Yasser Arafat turned his back on the armed struggle and embarked on the quest for a peaceful settlement to the 100-year-old conflict. Rabin, for his part, accepted the PLO as a partner to the talks and acknowledged the Palestinians as a people with national rights. Mutual denial was replaced by mutual recognition.

The historic reconciliation was based on a compromise: acceptance of the principle of the partition of Palestine. Both sides accepted territorial compromise as the basis for the settlement of their long and bitter conflict. Each side resigned itself to parting with territory it had previously regarded not only as its patrimony but as a vital part of its national identity. For the Palestinians the compromise they had to make was particularly painful. But by giving up their claim to 78% of mandatory Palestine they hoped to secure an independent state over the rest. The two sides, by accepting the principle of partition at the same time, seemed to be setting aside the ideological dispute over who was the rightful owner of Palestine and to be turning to the task of finding a practical solution to the problem of sharing the cramped living space between the River Jordan and the Mediterranean Sea.

The shape of the final settlement was not specified in the Declaration of Principles but left to negotiations between the two parties during the latter part of the transition period of five years. The declaration was completely silent on such vital issues as the right of return of the 1948 refugees, the borders of the Palestinian entity, the status of Jerusalem, and the future of the Jewish settlements in the occupied territories. Both sides took a calculated risk, realising that a great deal would depend on the way the experiment in Palestinian self-government worked out in practice. They assumed that the experience of working together during the transition period would generate the trust necessary to tackle the most difficult issues and to forge a viable peace settlement. Although the Declaration of Principles did not state specifically that there would be an independent Palestinian state at the end of the interim period, this was the clear intention of the leaders who signed it.

Not everyone on the Palestinian side shared these optimistic assumptions. Some Palestinian groups, secular as well as religious ones, rejected the very idea of compromise with the Jewish state. Others were more specific. Farouk Kaddumi, the 'foreign minister' of the PLO, argued that the deal compromised the basic national rights of the Palestinian people as well as the individual rights of the 1948 refugees. Hanan Ashrawi's first reaction was one of shock. It was clear to her that the PLO officials who negotiated the Oslo deal had not lived under occupation. She was deeply concerned by the gaps in the accord, the ambiguities and the lack of detail. She drew attention to the fact that the accord did not commit Israel to cease all settlement activity, that it postponed the question of Jerusalem, and that it said nothing about human rights.

Edward Said, the leading Palestinian intellectual, lambasted Yasser Arafat for unilaterally cancelling the *intifada*, for failing to coordinate his moves with the Arab states, and for introducing appalling disarray into the ranks of the PLO. 'The PLO,' he wrote, 'has transformed itself from a national liberation movement into a kind of small-town government, with the same handful of people still in command.' For the deal itself, Said had nothing but scorn. 'All secret deals between a very strong and a very weak partner necessarily involve concessions hidden in embarrassment by the latter,' he wrote. 'The deal before us', he continued, 'smacks of the PLO leadership's exhaustion and isolation, and of Israel's shrewdness.' 'Gaza and Jericho first . . . and last' was the poet Mahmoud Darwish's damning verdict on the deal.

The Oslo accord was greeted with dismay in nationalist Arab quarters: it was peace without justice or honour charged the critics. But it fell to the Arab world's most popular poet, Nizar Qabbani, to express the widespread opposition to the agreement. He did so in a prose poem, 'al-Muharwiluun' ('Those who rush or scurry'), which he wrote in London and published in 1995. Qabbani's bitter disappointment, and his anger with the PLO leaders who signed the accord, were given free reign:

> After this secret romance in Oslo
> we came out barren.
> They gave us a homeland
> smaller than a single grain of wheat
> a homeland to swallow without water
> like aspirin pills.
> Oh, we dreamed of a green peace
> and a white crescent
> and a blue sea.
> Now we find ourselves
> on a dung heap.

The history of the implementation of the Oslo accord has been one of endless delays on the Israeli side and of bitter disappointment on the Palestinian. Shimon Peres and Yossi Beilin, the Israeli architects of the accord, were sidelined after the signing ceremony. Their place at the negotiating table was taken by army officers who were critical of the security aspects of Oslo and who seemed intent not on ending the occupation but on repackaging it. They were willing to redeploy their troops from the big cities to the rural areas where resistance was more difficult to organise and clashes were less likely. But they were determined to retain as much control as possible for as long as possible in the occupied territories. And they managed to impose their own conception of the interim period: specific steps to transfer limited powers to the Palestinian Authority without giving up Israel's overall responsibility for security.

An Interim Agreement was signed by Rabin and Arafat on 28 September 1995, popularly known as Oslo II. It provided for elections to a Palestinian council, the transfer of legislative authority to this council, the withdrawal of Israeli forces from the Palestinian centres of population, and the division of the West Bank into three areas, A, B and C. Area A was placed under exclusive Palestinian control, area C under exclusive Israeli control; in area B, the Palestinian Authority (PA) exercised civilian power while Israel continued to be in charge

*Gaza, Israel: the first
prisoner to be released
after the Oslo agreement.
Credit: © Kai Wiedenhoeffer
/ Lookat / Network*

of security. Area A amounted to only four per cent of the area of the
West Bank, area B to another 25%; the rest was area C.

Oslo II, like Oslo I, was based on the assumption that the enmity
between the two warring tribes would subside during the transition
period, paving the way to an equitable final settlement. This did not
happen. On the contrary, the extremists on both sides did everything in
their power to undermine the agreement. There was a serious drop in
living standards on the West Bank and Gaza, partly as a result of frequent
Israeli border closures. Moreover, there was no significant gain in human
rights to compensate for the rise in unemployment, poverty and material
hardship. Human rights were continually sacrificed in the name of
'security' by both Israel and the PA. Worst of all, Jewish settlements
continued to be built on Palestinian land in palpable violation of the
spirit, if not the letter, of the Oslo accord.

In the Gaza Strip, home to just over 5,000 Jewish settlers, Israel
controlled a third of the land and most of the water resources desperately
needed by its one million Palestinian inhabitants. In the West Bank,
Israel retained control over the water resources and the lion's share of
the land. The building of settlements throughout the West Bank, and
especially around east Jerusalem, continued unabated and a network of
bypass roads seemed designed to pre-empt the possibility of Palestinian
statehood. In all these ways, the Oslo process actually worsened the

situation in the occupied territories and confounded Palestinian
aspirations to a state of their own.

Disappointment with Oslo and distrust of Israel deepened in the
wake of the Likud's electoral victory in May 1996. For Binyamin
Netanyahu, the new prime minister, was an ardent Jewish nationalist
and an unreconstructed proponent of the strategy of the iron wall.
Netanyahu was fiercely opposed to the Oslo accord because it recognised
the PLO, because it conceded that the Palestinian people had a
legitimate right to self-government and because it began the process of
partitioning western Palestine. In the lead-up to the election, opinion
polls showed that the majority of Israelis continued to support the policy
of gradual and controlled withdrawal from the occupied territories,
and that they were much less troubled by the prospect of a Palestinian
state alongside Israel than the politicians of the right. Consequently,
Netanyahu promised that, if elected, he would not renege on any of the
country's international commitments.

But this was precisely what he did after being elected by the
narrowest of margins. His three years in power consisted largely of
broken promises, deception, shabby manoeuvres, provocative acts like
the opening of the tunnel under the al-Aqsa Mosque and the building
of housing units on Arab land at Jabal Abu Ghrneim (Har Homa),
and endless delays. Netanyahu kept lecturing to the Palestinians about
reciprocity and acting unilaterally. He treated the PA not as an equal
partner but as a sub-contractor that was failing in its duty to uphold
Israel's security. Most galling of all to the Palestinians was Netanyahu's
failure to transfer to the PA 13% from Area C in accordance with the
Wye River Memorandum that he himself had signed on 22 October
1998. The one message that came across loud and clear was that the
Likud government was not prepared to end the occupation and that
it could not be trusted to keep agreements.

Ehud Barak won a decisive victory in the May 1999 election and
with it a clear mandate to resume and continue the peace process with
the Palestinians. But the difficulties and delays on the Palestinian track
persisted. Barak did not end Israeli violations of the Oslo accords. Under
his leadership, settlement activity was intensified, especially around
Jersualem. Palestinian prisoners were not released as agreed. The airport
at Gaza and the so-called 'safe passage' between Gaza and the West Bank
were opened but under strict and intrusive Israeli control. Jerusalem

remains closed to most Palestinians and travel between Palestinian towns is restricted by Israeli checkpoints. Seven years after the Oslo accord was signed, Israel retains full control over 61% of the West Bank and 20% of Gaza.

Negotiations on final status resumed but all the deadlines agreed by Ehud Barak and Yasser Arafat fell by the wayside. The basic problem was Barak's reluctance to proceed to a final status agreement in small steps, as envisaged at Oslo, and his preference for dealing with all the issues in one fell swoop. This is what Barak set out to achieve at the Camp David summit which Bill Clinton convened in July 2000 at his request. At the summit Barak presented Arafat with a package which included a demilitarised Palestinian state on 90% of the West Bank and Gaza, nominal concessions on the refugee issue, and Palestinian sovereignty over certain parts of east Jerusalem. Arafat rejected the package because the price tag attached to it was a formal renunciation of any outstanding Palestinian claims against the State of Israel. Arafat did not have the authority to accept this package even if he had wanted to. Thus, by insisting on a formal end to the dispute on terms that did not satisfy Palestinian national aspirations, Barak himself caused the collapse of the Camp David summit.

The collapse of the Camp David summit put the two sides on a collision course. Palestinian bitterness and frustration steadily mounted. Boycotts and closures of the Palestinian territories meant rising unemployment with disastrous social and economic consequences. Ariel Sharon's tour of Haram al-Sharif in the Old City of Jerusalem, on 28 September 2000, put the match to the barrel of gunpowder. By allowing this provocative tour against the advice of his security chiefs, Barak also assumed responsibility for the consequences. The most immediate consequence was violent clashes between Palestinian demonstrators and Israeli troops. In its first ten weeks, the *al-Aqsa intifada* resulted in about 280 Palestinian dead and over 8,000 wounded. The peace process may not be dead and buried as some observers claim, but it is certainly on hold until the guns fall silent. ❏

Avi Shlaim *is a fellow of St Antony's College and a professor of international relations at the University of Oxford. His book* The Iron Wall: Israel and the Arab World *recently appeared in paperback (Penguin)*

HELLA PICK

Time to remember

Jörg Haider's success forces Austria to confront its past

'Seven hundred years of anti-Semitism are enough,' proclaimed Vienna's mayor, Michael Haupl, shortly before Austria's stark Holocaust memorial to the 65,000 Austrian Jews killed during the Nazi era was unveiled at the end of October. At his side was Simon Wiesenthal, 'Nazi hunter' and director of the Jewish Documentation Centre in Vienna, who has dedicated his entire post-war life to the battle against forgetting or distorting the Holocaust, 'the greatest tragedy in history'. Austrians had not been alone in preferring to ignore the Shoah. But Austria's flirtation with its image as Hitler's 'first victim' – a distortion of fact widely interpreted as 'the Big Lie' – and the reluctance to acknowledge its considerable role in the Holocaust has been notorious, and Jörg Haider's political success has once again raised questions about the country's anti-Semitism and its political probity (*Index* 5/00).

The Holocaust Memorial, Rachel Whiteread's creation, is a white concrete rectangular cube. It has a dominant position in a small baroque square, the Judenplatz – Jews' Square – in the heart of Vienna. Beneath the square lie the remains of a medieval synagogue where hundreds of Jews perished in a pogrom against their community and immolated themselves rather than be forced into Catholicism in 1420/21. Simon Wiesenthal had long sought to expose the parallels between the Holocaust and those early attempts to eradicate Judaism. Austria had always preferred to distance itself from both.

Before the *Anschluss* in 1938, Austria had 190,000 Jews. Over one-third perished in the Holocaust, and most of the rest were forced to emigrate. Rachel Whiteread has encapsulated Jewish suffering in a sealed library, its books turned spine inward, with a door on one side which is hermetically closed. It symbolises the Nazis' destruction of Jewish books, and with it the attempt to destroy Jewish history and Jewish identity.

Judenplatz, Vienna:
Holocaust Memorial
by Rachel Whiteread.
Credit: Votava / PID

Beneath the door there is a simple inscription: 'In commemoration of 65,000 Austrian Jews who were killed by the Nazis between 1938 and 1945'. Around the other three sides of the memorial are the names of the concentration and extermination camps where Austria's Jews perished – often at the hands of Austrian Nazis. The list is long.

At the unveiling, Austria's President Klestil and Austria's Archbishop Cardinal Christoph Schonborn joined the Chief Rabbi in exhorting Austrians to accept responsibility for their role in the Holocaust and to discard anti-Semitism. The Cardinal spoke of 'Christianity's coresponsibility for the persecution of Jews', while President Klestil insisted that the nation must not ignore the fact that many Austrians had been involved in Nazi crimes. Austrians, he insisted, had been far too slow in dealing with their past. No more time must be lost. There was a coded message: Klestil has made no secret of his view that Haider's xenophobia was dangerous. 'Every sign of racism and anti-Semitism must be resolutely opposed.'

Completion of the Holocaust Memorial has provided official Austria with an important new opportunity to reinforce efforts to eradicate the mistakes of the past, and to create greater awareness of the need to confront difficult truths. The first attempt was made in 1991 by former Chancellor Vranitzki when he stood up in parliament with his landmark declaration to acknowledge Austria's moral responsibility for the participation of Austrians in the Nazi persecution of Jews.

Yet nine years later, Austria's friends in Europe and the United States again see cause for alarm after almost one-third of Austria's voters opted for a far-right party, the Freedom Party (FPÖ), which has become strong enough to secure inclusion in Austria's government. Even though Haider has not so far insisted on his participation in the federal cabinet, he has constantly sought to influence the government on foreign as well as domestic policies. During the ten months while the governments of the European Union maintained diplomatic sanctions against Austria, Haider exploited popular resentment to campaign against EU enlargement, arguing that it would unleash East European hordes on the long-suffering Austrian nation.

With the sanctions lifted, Haider's standing in Austria is much reduced. He is embroiled in a dirty-tricks scandal, in which he personally, as well as his party, is alleged to have obtained police files to discredit rival political figures. Public opinion polls show that the Freedom Party has lost substantially since last year's federal elections, and is once again well behind Austria's two mainstream parties, the Social Democrats and the People's Party.

But even if one accepts – as most analysts do – that a substantial proportion of the Freedom Party's support in the 1999 election came from disgruntled voters who wanted to break up a deeply embedded power structure, Haider still has a hard-core following for whom he represents an escape from past as well as contemporary reality. Such people believe that the pressure on Austrians to acknowledge a less than honourable role during the Nazi era only serves to reinforce a sense of victimhood.

Austrians did not invent their victim image. The four wartime allies were initially responsible. The description of Austria as Hitler's 'First Victim' occurs in the 1943 Moscow Declaration. The allies added a proviso that Austria must accept responsibility for its 'participation in the war on Hitler's side'. But this was scrapped – at Austrian insistence –

*Vienna, March 1938: photographed through a coffee-shop window,
cheering crowds celebrate the* Anschluss. *Credit: AKG*

from the preamble to the 1955 State Treaty which restored full
sovereignty to Austria. The assertion that Austria had been Hitler's
first victim was, however, retained. Obviously this reinforced Austria's
preferred image of itself as an innocent victim of Nazi aggression.

Austria's leadership in the early post-war period included several who
had themselves been in concentration camps and perceived themselves as
victims. They shared with their cabinet colleagues a desire to play down
the magnitude of Nazi crimes in the interests of creating unity and a
renewed sense of identity for Austria.

Cabinet minutes of that era also reveal a shocking degree of anti-
Semitism, even from men with an established anti-Nazi record. They
were far more intent on restoring the civil rights of former Nazis, and
of compensating returning Austrian prisoners-of-war who had fought
in the Wehrmacht, than in addressing restitution measures for the Jewish
victims of Nazi persecution.

Nazi Party members were excluded from Austria's first post-war election. But the 500,000 former Nazis had their voting rights restored in time for the next election in 1949. The two mainstream parties competed with each other to woo the 'Union of Independents', as the precursor of the Freedom Party called itself. The Socialists even channelled secret funds to the Freedom Party (which was formed in 1955). In 1970 Chancellor Bruno Kreisky amended Austria's electoral law in the Freedom Party's favour as part of a deal to secure its support for his minority government.

Denazification was never high on Austria's post-war agenda and the Occupation powers, preoccupied with the Cold War, not only lost interest but even recruited former Austrian Nazis as informers. The Church made no attempt to appeal to conscience. Teachers, judges and civil servants remained in place without much effort to question their record. War crimes trials were much less prominent than in Germany; and, more often than not, the accused were declared innocent.

For much of the time, Simon Wiesenthal was beating a lonely path against what amounted to a virtual conspiracy by Austria's political elites to suppress the past. He had started in 1945 with a campaign to secure evidence of Nazi crimes from survivors in the displaced persons camps. After gaining worldwide fame for his role in finding Adolf Eichmann, Wiesenthal settled in Vienna where he established his Documentation Centre as a vehicle to bring Nazi criminals to justice.

Appalled by Austria's efforts to whitewash its behaviour during the Nazi era, Wiesenthal compiled a compelling document on Austria's culpability. He took from 1963 to 1966 to construct his dossier of Austrian involvement with the Nazis. Even though Austria only comprised 8.5% of 'Greater' Germany's population, Wiesenthal claimed he had strong evidence that Austrians had been responsible for the extermination of three million people – half the estimated victims of the Holocaust. His document also revealed the extent to which former Nazis remained in control of Austria's administrative machinery.

Austria's Chancellor in 1966, Dr Josef Klaus, ignored Wiesenthal's evidence and, far from winning public support, Wiesenthal was widely accused of seeking to give Austria a bad name. Undeterred, he argued that Austria had a duty to press on with war crimes trials. 'Otherwise Austria will be guilty of leaving an empty space in history, and this will leave a stigma for all times.'

Austria's leaders – and the general public – remained deaf to these arguments for almost three more decades. Bruno Kreisky was Chancellor from 1970 to 1983. The fact that he was a Jew did not spur him on to tackle the war crimes or restitution issues more emphatically. Like his predecessors he preferred to draw a line under the past, and to adopt a policy of all-inclusiveness.

In the end, it was the international outcry, on account of his wartime record, against the election of Kurt Waldheim as head of state that finally drove Austria's political leaders to realise that Austria would only recover its good name if it abandoned the Big Lie and demonstrated its acceptance of moral responsibility for past behaviour. Even then, it came at a snail's pace. Waldheim was elected in 1986 and, though Chancellor Vranitzki was advised to act swiftly, it took him until 1991 to decide that Austria was ready to take stock of its involvement in the Holocaust.

However, once the decision was taken, Vranitzki did follow it up with practical measures. Restitution was speeded up; pensions were given to all émigrés who had been forced to leave Austria after the *Anschluss*; a fund was set up for survivors. At last Austria wanted to show that it was capable of fairness to the victims of the Holocaust.

Vranitzki's successors have pursued the same policies. Many works of art have been restored to their former owners [though there is a renewed controversy over pictures in the national collection as we go to press, *Ed.*]. An agreement to pay compensation for forced labour has recently been agreed. An international team of historians is at work to establish an accurate record of Austria's recent past.

Jörg Haider's rise to political stardom has invigorated Holocaust debate. Even if some of his supporters believe the international community is once again victimising Austria, there are many others who contend that his presence on the political scene merely underlines the importance of remembering the Holocaust and understanding Austria's involvement in Nazi atrocities.

Vienna's new Holocaust memorial is more than a symbol of remembrance. It is also intended as a perpetual call to the Austrian conscience. ❑

Hella Pick is former diplomatic editor of the Guardian, *and author of the recently published* Guilty Victim – Austria from the Holocaust to Haider *(IB Tauris)*

GÜNTER GRASS

I remember

Whenever we make our plans for the future, the past has left its mark on what we thought was virgin territory; it has set up signposts that just lead us back to what we have already lived through

I remember . . . or else perhaps there is something which makes me remember, something which runs through my being, leaving behind its smell, or something which was hiding, sheltering in old letters, just waiting to be reawakened by some sly little word. It's a kind of trap, one of a number of things that can make us stumble. Something emerges from this background world, something to which we can at once put a name. Mute objects come to meet us, things which had been lying dormant around us for years – or so we thought – reveal their secrets. It can be a bit of a nuisance! There are dreams as well, dreams in which we fail to recognise ourselves, which we cannot grasp, but which demand to be interpreted and constantly reinterpreted.

Even when we are travelling through places that we have left behind, places which have been destroyed or lost, which sound unfamiliar or have names that are new, even then we may suddenly be seized by a memory. That is what happened to me in the spring of 1958 when I visited the city of Gdansk for the first time since the war, as it slowly emerged from its heaps of rubble, and I hoped that here and there I might come across some surviving trace of what Danzig had once been.

Sure enough, the schools were still where they had been, and that characteristic school smell still infested the corridors. But the journey to school seemed shorter than I remembered it. Then I set off to find Brösen, which used to be a fishing village, and I found that the Baltic lapped against it as gently as it ever had. Suddenly I was standing outside the closed bathing station, beside the entrance next to the kiosk, likewise chained and padlocked. And all in a moment I could feel once more the thrill of one of the modest pleasures of my childhood: lemonade crystals tasting of strawberry, lemon and lily of the valley; you could buy them in sachets in the kiosk for a few pfennigs. But the minute this refreshing drink began to sparkle in my memory, it began to stir up stories, real deceitful stories, which had been waiting, needing only a single word of recognition to bring them to the surface. This simple, innocuous lemonade powder, meant to be dissolved in water, set off a chain reaction in my brain: that first trembling love, that sparkle, repeated over and over, but never experienced.

A recollection, no matter how deeply buried or fragmentary it may be, is more than just a matter of forcing your memory to work with precision. A recollection is allowed to cheat, to embellish or to pretend, whereas the memory is happy to be seen as a scrupulously trustworthy accountant. However, we know that powers of memory diminish with age, whereas recollections of all that had long been buried, recollections of childhood, now seem to come closer and often cluster around moments of happiness.

Although I'm still fond of going out to look for mushrooms, even today I am taken unawares by the sudden memory of a moment when, as I child, I used to go off into the Kaszubska forest and suddenly came across a single cep. It was bigger and a more magnificent specimen than any that I've found since, and so I keep looking. Recollection provides me with the measure of what to look for.

When it comes to recollection, the writer is a past master. Since narrative is what he writes, he has been trained in the craft. He knows that recollection is like a cat that has to be stroked – sometimes in the wrong direction – until it starts to tremble and then it will begin to purr. This is how he uses his own recollections and, when needed, the recollections of people whom he invents as fancy takes him. Recollection is his quarry, his compost heap, his archive. He nurtures it as carefully as if it were a second crop.

Of course he is aware that literature is a greedy beast, prepared to gulp down even newspaper articles and reports before they are at all ripe, before they have been licked into shape; but when the lean years come, chewed-over recollections are his staple diet, he recalls memories that have already been raked over once. Perhaps it goes with the job, this ability to turn painful or shameful moments or even the memory of some past failure into something that has entertainment value.

That is why my lost homeland is something that forces recollection upon me, imposes an obligation to write out of obsession. That homeland, lost for ever, which has left a void that cannot be filled by a substitute, by some ersatz homeland or other, had to be recalled once more and then exorcised, banished on to paper, sheet after sheet and, though shattered, it had to find its reflection in a shard from a broken mirror. The recollection had to be drawn off in a way so carefully measured as to keep a narrator supplied with great cupfuls of it, quenching his thirst for his former self, allowing him to use his own particular perspective to see as great that which was small, to see as small that which was great. Every sluice gate is opened. The tramlines of Danzig, the cinemas in the old town and in the working-class districts. In recollection, the image of that Kashubian uncle seems quite different. He was a man who, at the beginning of the war, had been reluctant to be declared a hero for his defence of the Polish post office. When he died, the family said nothing. There was only chatter about blockades, special communiqués, continual victories, banal, everyday events drawn out endlessly, and all that remained of these were scraps of words that hung in the air.

Rebuilding Dresden, 1946. Credit: Hulton Getty Picture Collection Ltd

There was the language: a patois that would die out a few decades after the end of the war with the oldest of the refugees, a *Plattdeutsch* that would be pushed further and further back into East and West Prussia. The Kashubian version of it I heard when my family spoke German has remained in my memory down to the finest detail. I remember, for example, what an aunt whispered in my ear in 1958, something that loses in the translation into standard German: '*Ech waiss, Ginterchen, em Wasten is basser, aber em Osten is scheener* (Günter, love, I know the West is better, but the East is more beautiful).' This carefully balanced summing-up has not only stuck in my memory but, what is much more, it still runs through my books, weighing up the East and the West, and still today gives me a perspective on them.

That's enough of 'professional recollection', the phrase that sums up the writer's obsession. But there is also such a thing as collective memory. Throughout Europe it serves as a pretext: you either strive to evoke it or you refrain from doing so. Wars and war crimes are laid at its door. There are entire ideological frameworks that it cannot shake off. This is particularly true of the still painful collective memory of the previous generation.

Perhaps that is why we Germans had the idea of coining a neologism as hackneyed as 'the duty of remembrance'. It is required as 'admission of responsibility' and rejected as insulting, and this is all done conscientiously: for decades now, for as long as the past has constantly caught up with us, it has been carried out as if it were a duty, since the 1960s, even by what was then the younger generation, the one which we used to term 'uncompromised'. It is as if children and grandchildren wanted to do the remembering in place of their parents and grandparents who remain silent. Not a week passes that we are not warned about the dangers of forgetting. Once we have sufficiently fulfilled expectations by remembering the Jews who were persecuted, forced to emigrate, murdered in immeasurably large numbers, as an afterthought we remember the murder of 10,000 Gypsies. And now, much too late according to many people, we are forced to remember what happened to thousands of forced labourers who came from Poland, from the Soviet Union and many other countries to take their places on the production lines in factories working for the German war effort.

It is as if the crimes carried out over a period of just 12 years take on more and more weight the further we move in time from deeds which all the world recognises as shameful. Attempts to give concrete form to recollection by means of memorials seem doomed to failure. In Berlin, for example, conflict broke out, and it wasn't only matters of aesthetics that loomed large. 'Remember!' cried one side; 'Enough!' the other side shouted back. It happens that foreigners, observing the Germans' dealings with their past, speak of 'self-flagellation', which makes the point that a process of recollection is a torture. But there is really no end in sight. Whenever we make our plans for the future, the past has left its mark on what we thought was virgin territory; it has set up signposts that just lead us back to what we have already lived through.

It is always strange and disturbing to hear it said that it is only ever late in the day and with much hesitation that the sufferings inflicted on the Germans during the war are recalled. The consequences of the war, begun without scruple and criminally pursued – that is, the destruction of German towns, the deaths of thousands of civilians as a result of bombing, the expulsion and distress of the 12 million Germans in the East who had to flee: all this was only ever mentioned as a background. In post-war literature, the memory of the many who died in the nights of bombing and the mass exodus was never reflected in the same way. Experience shows that victims of violence, whoever was responsible for it, do not wish to remember the atrocities they have undergone.

And so many things remain unsaid, even when they keep forcing themselves into our consciousness like painful memories. Since there never really was a peace, since, in the Balkans, in the Caucasus, in so many theatres of horror around the world, the present is given over to murder, to evacuation and deportation, then recollection, the echo of the sufferings we have lived through, will never cease.

Recently, the Hungarian writer György Konrad wrote about Europe: 'To remember is human, we could even say that it is the essence of humanity.' While Nature treats history with indifference, it is, he insists, a specific human characteristic to be able to remember in two ways, as if this ability were both a benefit and a curse. It is a curse because it will not leave us in peace and a benefit because it overcomes death. Thus, in recollection, we may speak with both the living and the dead. As long as we are remembered, we live on. Forgetting puts the seal on death. ❏

Günter Grass won the Nobel Prize for Literature in 1999. His latest book, Die Gedichte 1955–1986, is due out in early 2001

ALESSANDRO PORTELLI

Fearful symmetry

The event

On 25 March 1944, newspapers in Rome carried a press release from the German command:

> In the afternoon of the 23 March 1944, criminal elements carried out an attack, by throwing bombs at a German police column which was passing along the Via Rasella. In consequence of this attack, 32 German policemen were killed and several wounded. The German Command, therefore, has given orders that for every German killed, ten Badoglio-Communist criminals will be shot. This order has already been carried out.

The order was carried out at the Fosse Ardeatine (Ardentine Caves), a sand quarry on the periphery of the city. The final number of men executed was 335, a further German soldier having died the following day. It was not the worst crime committed by Nazis in Europe, in Italy (Marzabotto and Sant'Anna di Stazzema claimed more victims), or even in Rome (of 1,022 Jews deported on 16 October 1943, only 17 returned; hundreds more died in later deportations). Yet the event at the Fosse Ardeatine retains a powerful and controversial hold on collective memory and imagination, far in excess of mere numbers.

The massacre at the Fosse Ardeatine took place in a city of huge symbolic value: not only was this the capital of Italy, it was the seat of the Catholic Church and a city redolent with history. The caves are opposite the catacombs, the scene of early Christian martyrdoms, an analogy not lost on subsequent commentators.

The massacre covered all classes, religions and political persuasions. Recent immigrants to the city from the countryside as well as old-established groups like the Jews, who had lived in the city since the time of Julius Caesar, and the descendants of old local communities, like the Trastevere artisan Enrico Ferola whose father had fought with Garibaldi

in the 1860s, were affected. So were members of the military loyal to
the king, communists, Christian Democrats, Liberals, Socialists – even
disaffected former fascists such as Aldo Finzi, a former secretary of state
in Mussolini's first cabinet. There were 75 Jews, a priest, many practising
Catholics, at least 15 Freemasons, atheists. No part of the city or the
provinces was spared: the impact was felt throughout the country and
extended through networks of family, neighbourhoods, workplaces,
schools, parishes, unions, parties. For myself alone, there were Pilo
Albertelli, my mother's philosophy teacher; Angelo and Alfredo Capecci,
who grew up in the neighbourhood where I now live; Ivano Scarioli,
the uncle of a student whose dissertation I supervised. I collected dozens
of stories from students and colleagues without even leaving my office.

The majority of those killed were involved in some way with the
Resistance; others were taken because they were Jews or because they
happened to be in the wrong place at the wrong time – Ettore Ronconi,
for instance, a wine merchant from the Alban hills who had been exiled
as a communist years earlier, was delivering wine to a restaurant; the
Pignotti and Mastrangeli families, who owned a shop around the corner,
had been denounced by a neighbour for not attending the 'Fascist
Saturday' rally. Others, finally, were merely rounded up at random in the
Regina Coeli jail when the Nazis feared they would not have enough
prisoners to make up the number. No single story, no single label covers
them all.

The term 'victim' is rejected by many of their survivors because it
denies their commitment to the Resistance. No collective term describes
these people as a whole. Even 'Italians' is inadequate: 11 were foreigners.
Complex identities and widespread involvement, as well as the symbolic
power of place, have ensured this story retains its hold on the
imagination.

The narrative

In most neighbourhoods of Rome, from the historic centre to the
working-class peripheries, visitors are likely to come across plaques
commemorating victims of the Fosse Ardeatine massacre, often
denouncing in graphic terms the horror of Nazi 'barbarity' or 'savagery'.

Yet this was no wild, uncontrolled, impromptu orgy of killing in the
heat of battle. The massacre was organised in a thoroughly organised way

with all the bureaucratic efficiency and attention to detail typical of a modern state. The fearful symmetry of 'ten Italians for one German' typifies this behaviour; that the executioners miscalculated and killed five victims too many signifies their underlying confusion and panic.

No sooner had the attack taken place in via Rasella than the Germans responded with plans to punish the city: deport 1,000 people, destroy the whole neighbourhood. Hitler's early orders were less extreme: execute 50 Italians for each German. The SS commander Herbert Kappler and the German consul Eithel Friedrich Möllhausen finally negotiated it down to ten for one, claiming that they would only execute prisoners who had already been sentenced to death. Kappler and Möllhausen later claimed this as evidence of their humanitarian concern.

When Kappler went to check his records, however, he found he had only three people under sentence of death. He spent the night at his desk, like any dutiful bureaucrat with a deadline to meet and a quota to fill, gradually expanding his criteria of inclusion: those accused of 'crimes' punishable with death; those sentenced to above 15 years; those liable to sentences above 15 years. When his quota was still unfulfilled, he added all the Jews he had at hand – 'rather than Italians, whose guilt was harder to prove', he explained later – and, finally and at random, anyone unfortunate enough to be in the local jail that night.

It was of the essence that the retaliation should take place immediately, to cow the city and impress it with the invincibility of German power. Given their number, there would be no time to execute the victims in the traditional manner by firing squad and with clergy present at the death. It was necessary to identify a 'natural mass grave', as Kappler put it, where the victims could be dispatched collectively and quickly. One of Kappler's officers suggested the caves on the via Ardeatina. The prisoners were transported silently and efficiently through the city, miles from the centre, further evidence (if any were needed) that this was no sudden explosion of rage. Once there, they were led into the caves in groups of five, while officers and men took turns behind them with machine guns. Some of his men were reluctant or sick; Kappler comforted them like a father and helped them do their duty. When the floor of the caves was covered with bodies, fresh batches of victims were forced to kneel on top of their dead companions.

Kappler explained at his trial that he denied his victims the comfort of clergy only because, with time so short, he felt it would be painful to tear victims and confessors apart; 'out of concern for the physical and psychological well-being' of the victims, he said, he ordered them to be shot at point-blank range. Even so, there were those who did not die instantly and were left in agony beneath the bodies of the dead.

Only a week after the massacre, the head of the Fascist Party in Rome, Giuseppe Pizzirani, told his members the retaliation might have been avoided had the partisans of via Rasella turned themselves in as the Germans demanded. This is the first documented occurrence of what was to become the commonplace narrative of events in the via Rasella–Fosse Ardeatine: the creation of an anti-partisan mythology, in which bills were posted all over the city and repeated radio broadcasts appealed to the partisans to turn themselves in and prevent reprisals on the population. The German press release, however, tells a different tale, one the Nazi commanders reluctantly confirmed in their post-war trials: the retaliation was announced only after it had been carried out.

The memory

All this has been a matter of public record for half a century. Yet the facts have been obscured by popular beliefs and narratives based on ignorance and misinformation. These put the blame for the massacre on the partisans rather than the Germans: it was the 'irresponsible' attack of the former and their refusal to turn themselves in that led to all the trouble. This belief is allegedly a 'grassroots' version of history as opposed to the 'official' one and was fostered and disseminated by influential institutions – the media, the Church – at the centre of public life. It has the seduction of an alternative history but one that is endorsed by the highest authority.

An early version of events that put things in this light was formulated by the official newspaper of the Catholic Church, the *Osservatore Romano*. Along with the political right, the Catholic media and sources close to the Church were to play a major part in perpetuating this version over the years, allowing it to seep into the public imagination and poison not only the memory of the event, but with it the memory of the Resistance, of the identity and origins of the Republic.

Other factors contributed to the credibility of the alternative version of history outside its obvious ideological constituency. The myth of Rome as an 'open city' – never recognised or respected as such either

by the Allies or by the Germans – erases the memory of the violence of
the German occupation, the thousands of people deported, the dozens
of political prisoners executed, the massacres perpetrated before and after
via Rasella without partisan 'provocation'; it wipes out the knowledge
that via Rasella was no sudden breach of the peace but one of more than
40 partisan attacks, many of which had resulted in German casualties,
none of which had elicited this type of retaliation.

The desperate need to believe that something could have been done
and the sheer horror of the massacre make it easier to shift the discourse
to the attack in via Rasella rather than contemplate what happened in
the caves. In peacetime, it is harder to remember that the aim of the
Germans (mythically 'stern but just') was not simply to punish a group
of transgressors, but to terrorise and subdue the city with a display of
military and political might. Finally, the lapse of political and ideological
tension in the transition from war to a difficult peace, especially in
the gathering Cold War climate, makes the partisan action look like
the unauthorised intervention of private citizens rather than the
continuation of legitimate urban guerrilla activity. A 'perfect' narrative,
corroborated by influential channels, met an audience ready to receive
it. This was the ultimate success of the German retaliation.

The story is usually told as a self-enclosed sequence of partisan
attack and German retaliation. But it begins much earlier, with the
establishment of Rome as the national capital and with memories of the
Risorgimento: Rosario Bentivegna, who fired the fuse in via Rasella, was
the grandson of Sicilian patriots executed in the 1830s and 1850s. And
it continues, long after the order has been carried out, in the lives of the
survivors.

The one thing that the dead of the Fosse Ardeatine have in common
is gender: they were all men. This leaves the rest of the story in the
hands of women – mothers, wives, daughters, sisters – who are charged
with mourning and survival.

After the liberation of Rome, the Allied authorities suggested that,
since the bodies were already 'buried' (the Germans had blown up the
caves), the best thing would be to concrete the place over and build a
monument on top.

'So, that's where my mother steps in,' says Vera Simoni, daughter of
the air force general Simone Simoni, killed at the Fosse Ardeatine. 'My
mother said, "No: I want recognition for each and every one." We went

to see General Pollock, the head of the Allied Forces, and my mother said: "Look, we came to tell you that we know you want to make this monument and we refuse to accept it; we want identification, body by body.'"

One reason why the memory of the Fosse Ardeatine has remained so vivid is that the pain of the survivors had time to freeze into shape before they could mourn. It was months before the families were sure that their loved ones were at the caves, and even longer before they could actually recognise the bodies. It takes a body to cry over and care for, a ritual, a burial for death to be rationalised and accepted in some way. But these bodies had to be unburied before they could be buried, and the process was harrowing.

The pathologist Attilio Ascarelli, who carried out the exhumation and identification, visited the caves in the middle of summer, when the corpses had been underground for three months. He writes: 'Among the miserable scattered limbs insects swarmed, thousands of larvae fed on the tortured, broken flesh, and huge rats swarmed around among the unburied and untended remains and shattered skulls.' This is the scene that confronted the survivors, women and children, as they identified their loved ones and supervised their burial in the place where they had died.

At a time when it was still not accepted, these women were forced to go out to work to support themselves and their families. They took whatever unskilled jobs they could get in the public sector in Rome – state printing offices, tobacco plants, hospitals, cleaning jobs. Young wives nursed their children with anger and despair in their milk; hardly any of them remarried, and none successfully. They made the rounds of public institutions and welfare offices to secure their war widows' pensions, and had to go through humiliations and sexual harassment they had never encountered and had no name to describe. They sensed that the city pitied them, but did not want them around as reminders of the deaths.

Ada Pignotti was 23 when her husband was killed. She believes the swift shift of attention from the massacre to the placing of blame on the partisans was a way of exorcising their presence and what they stood for. The women supported each other, shared their grief and common struggle for survival and justice. Meanwhile, the children grew up surrounded by pain – sometimes obsessive, in other cases unspoken and more oppressive. With their mothers working, many had to spend years in institutions where they suffered emotional and material deprivation.

Gabriella Polli was three when her father died. She was one of four daughters. Her mother worked nights as a phone operator, days as a seamstress, cleaned house and looked after them. Twenty years later, she called her mother one night: '"What are you doing, Mum?" She said, "I'm crying because, you know, after 30 years now I have time to cry for your dad." I was stunned. She said, "Yes, because now that I'm left alone, now I've retired, I'm remembering my poor Domenico; now I'm crying for him. I never had the time before." Terrible. My mother always said, "I don't have time, my dears, to sit down and cry. Around here, everyone cries. But I have to go; I have to run." How could a woman sit in the house and cry? What would she eat, bread and tears? These widows couldn't cry. It was impossible; they had to run.'

It was a strange grief, an absent grief, a grief that wasn't there. A grief that was washed white, pressed, darned, folded, insulted. ❑

Alessandro Portelli *teaches at Rome's La Sapienza University. His book on the massacre,* L'Ordine è già stato eseguito: Roma, le Fosse Ardeatine, la memoria *(Donzelli, 1999) won the Viareggio Book Prize for non-fiction in 1999*

GASPAR TAMÁS

The tanks
of oblivion

Old-style dissidents, who fought communism in its prime, find they are not the heroes they might have been. They embarrass the old enemy who now sits in the halls of democracy and are a reproach to those who did nothing to oppose the old rulers – but now find they don't much care for the new system either

Six years ago, I asked in *The Times Literary Supplement* why everyone so hated the dissidents; then I tried a little self-criticism of erstwhile dissenters, something most people were too polite to attempt. I was naive, perhaps, in attributing our unpopularity to our own failings. As I look at the subject again today, it seems more likely to have been our success in helping create the new society; the fresh-minted liberal capitalism that most of our fellow citizens have come to loathe.

Liberal capitalism has arrived, with all its familiar trappings: parliamentary democracy, ideological pluralism, freedom of expression, graft, greed, tabloid television, vulgar public discourse, and so on. To the casual western observer it may look vaguely familiar and, since we had no other ideas to offer in its place, it was indeed the nebulous western model that was deemed to have won the great battle.

Nevertheless, there is a world of difference between Dutch and Guatemalan democracy, just as there was between Swedish and Cambodian socialism. In the former Soviet bloc, from Vladivostok to East Berlin, most people think the new order bears more resemblance to a natural disaster than to an orderly social change planned in advance. After the collapse of the former system (the main characteristics of which are still baffling theorists and analysts) there was no other recourse than to look abroad. The time was not right for Utopias based on the modest aspiration of local people taking control of their own destiny.

The result was a Frankenstein's monster: a bit of German constitutional jurisprudence, a little of US civil rights, some French presidentialism, a chunk of Westminster parliamentarianism, a wee bit of Swiss referenda, some Chicago monetarism, a dollop of Austrian xenophobia and party-bound civil service, etc., etc. Everyone spoke of a mechanism that would 'work'; very few seemed to care about, or believe in, what was 'just' or 'fair'. In most East European languages, the words are simply not current today.

Budapest, November 1956: Hungarian dissidents wave the national tricolour from a Soviet tank captured in the main square in front of the houses of parliament. Credit: AP

At a conference of philosophy teachers in Hungary recently, I was asked to explain the difference between 'true' and 'just' (they are etymologically linked in Hungarian). A Romanian participant asked me whether 'justice' had any meaning other than its legal sense as in 'jurisprudence' or 'judiciary'. If the idea of justice had ever impinged on people's understanding of life generally, for instance in matters such as taxation, redistribution, profit, cultural equality, collective action, these linguistic problems could not have happened.

Our democratic change is considered a disaster: the result of anonymous social and political forces, of the inability of 'state socialism' to compete in the world market or deal with discontent at home. The most articulate and militant anti-establishment movement in eastern Europe, Solidarity in Poland, combined a demand for free expression and free elections with a rejection of free-market competition. The Polish workers wanted a well-planned welfare state, full employment and regular pay rises – like workers everywhere, always. Nobody wanted an end to free health care, free education, state pensions, rent control, free kindergarten; simply that the quality and funding of the social services be improved, and control handed over to civil society. Neo-liberal economists argued that all this was impossible given the bankruptcy of the state. But, unlike their counterparts in the English-speaking world, they did not preach the virtues of self-reliance, thrift and self-improvement. American neo-conservatives believe welfare claimants are immoral; the new East European elites think they are merely troublesome and hopeless – and usually 'coloured', like the Roma (Gypsies), for instance.

The 'new democracy' seemed like just one more instance of shenanigans at the top: a new ploy by the bosses to save their skins and pacify the restless natives. Nevertheless, it opened new opportunities of advocacy, new chances to voice grudges and destroy enemies, all of which our societies used skilfully, without believing for a minute in any intrinsic value. The fundamental metaphor of the 'side entrance' (*kiskapu*, literally 'small door') in Hungary is a good one: if you cannot enter the house of the state or public affairs by the main gates, you can bribe your way in through some inconspicuous hatch or cat flap. Liberal democracy appeared as a legitimation of the 'side entrance'.

The dissident cult of civil society and civil disobedience did not prepare people for the crucial distinction made in 'modern' societies

*Budapest, 1956: Stalin toppled. The uprising was brutally crushed
by the USSR after 11 days of fighting. Credit: AP*

between the formal and the informal; between group interest and the
public good. The dominant language in the new democracies of eastern
Europe is that of interest, advantage, compromise and consent. Moral
criticism is viewed as something akin to godless Bolshevism. Public
interest is always expressed as a compound of special interests: the
negative connotation of 'special interests', as in the US, for example,
never took root – no more than social justice as the common interest
of society at large, or our common interest in living in a society
governed by some sort of moral order. We have only a certain nostalgia
for a moral order now irretrievably lost.

Justice, fairness and equality seen only as aspects of a fictitious past is
dangerous and people forget how terrible, unjust and unfree the Soviet-

type dictatorships were. They are viewed today as failed experiments in social justice, as the hopelessness of all collective, as opposed to individual endeavour. One result of this is that almost all anti-discriminatory movements – trade unions, anti-racist and feminist movements and the like – are weak.

East European governments do not even deny that their aim is a periodic redistribution of spoils; 'progressive' and 'liberal' intellectuals often regarded it as an encouraging sign of democracy that every four years or so there is a new gang at the helm that is sufficiently motivated by political alternation as to leave something for the others to nick. If you are patient enough, there will be a 'side entrance' for everyone – now for the right, now for the left – provided the PR and spin are up to it.

All this, of course, is not uncommon in western democracies either. The main difference, though, is that in the West this view does not obscure the whole horizon; there are living traditions of resistance; of dissent that is more than mere discontent. In other words, there exists a critical tradition.

This tradition in eastern Europe is equated with varieties of Marxism, now the synonym of failure and defeat. The critical tradition has lost its philosophical edge in the West too, but survives in somewhat contradictory rainbow coalitions like, for instance, the protest movements in Seattle, Washington, Prague and London. The philosophical and moral foundations of, say, Reclaim the Streets, are not spelled out, but there is a tacit consensus on their aims among activists.

This consensus is impossible in the former Soviet bloc since any possible sources are poisoned by Stalin, Mao and their successors – the only kind of genuine, indigenous variant of modernisation our region has ever known. Our – the 'dissidents' – rights-based critique of 'communism' proved highly unsatisfactory. For historical reasons easy enough to understand, it had to be anarchic and individualistic, topped with the the preachy, high-falutin moral self-righteousness à la Havel. (Examine the behaviour of Czech police during the recent anti-IMF protests in Prague. There's 'radical tolerance'.)

Colonial societies are wont to wallow in defeat. This usually results in a denial of responsibility, brilliantly described by VS Naipaul. Societies that only *feel* colonial are much the same. East Europeans believe they cannot change anything important since the present state of affairs has been preordained by superior forces they can neither influence nor mollify. These forces consist in the 'system' itself. It denies justly deserved benefits on the grounds of a mythical lack of funds, as does the West with its armadas and its millions.

We are permanently relegated to the 'side entrance'. Here we can embroider on our long-acquired oriental wiles and make them more contemporary, more with it, cool even. But it is scarcely our place and station to carp where the grand designs of the truly great are concerned. Like Sancho Panzo, Figaro and the good soldier Shweik, we shall, however, deceive our masters. ❑

Gaspar Tamás is research professor at the Institute of Philosophy, Hungarian Academy of Sciences, Budapest

ELIE KAGAN

Massacre in the city

The events of 17 October 1961, when up to 40,000 Algerian
nationalists, defying a curfew, took to the streets of Paris in peaceful
protest against the prolonged war in their country (1956–62) and in
support of independence, have long been a subject of controversy and
concealment.

As night fell over the City of Light that day, the streets were
spattered with blood; the river choked with the corpses of murdered
demonstrators as riot police under the authority of the city's *préfet,*
Maurice Papon, launched into the crowd with batons and live
ammunition. Papon had ordered them to 'shoot on sight'.

Official figures released by the authorities at the time stated that just
two people had died; as late as 1997, this was revised to 'several dozen'.
Eyewitnesses told a different story: about 200 Algerians were killed on
the spot; as many more of the 10,000 taken into police custody simply
vanished. Two weeks after the massacre, bodies that had been dumped
in the Seine were still being washed ashore downstream.

It is only now, 40 years after the event, that it is once more in the
public eye – and photographic evidence of the slaughter made public.
Attention has been focused on the growing national debate by the
opening of the Algerian war archives, showing irrefutable evidence
of torture by French troops during the War of Independence, and by
Maurice Papon's 1997–98 trial for crimes against humanity in WWII
(see p43), which revived interest in his role in the events of 1961.

Why so long? It is a sorry tale of suppression and censorship, a story
in which the French authorities, smarting from their losses in Algeria
and the failure of peace negotiations, treated all Algerians with
contempt. Too few voices then spoke of the racism, abuse and violation

of human rights in what was by any colonial standards a particularly brutal war – and no one was listening.

Every attempt was made to ensure no evidence of the massacre got out. Of all the photographers present at the time, only one got his work out. Most had their film confiscated by police; others it seems, among them the photographer for the communist *L'Humanité*, had their work destroyed by their own editors.

Elie Kagan, a left-wing photo-journalist, hid his camera in a pile of rubbish, to which he returned once the fracas had died down. Although the pictures survived the police search they remained unpublished; as recently as 1996, copies of the Algerian daily *Liberté* carrying the pictures were seized by customs officers in Lyons. Only now are they gaining proper exposure.

In 1999, Kagan's pictures were unavailable for inclusion in 'Underexposed' (*Index* 6/1999), a history of censored photographs. 'There's no such thing,' we were told. The following selection is from the 20 or so surviving Kagan pictures.

DG

Paris, 17 October 1961: Concorde metro station
Riot police line up some of the 10,000
demonstrators taken into custody. Many
Algerians sought sanctuary from the bullets on
underground platforms, only to be rounded up
and escorted en masse to the cells

Paris, 17 October 1961: Solferino metro station
A student member of the Partie Socialiste
Unifée hands out metro tickets to Algerian
demonstrators escaping the violence
on the streets

Paris, 17 October 1961: rue des Pâquerettes Nanterre
A battered victim, blood pouring from
multiple head wounds

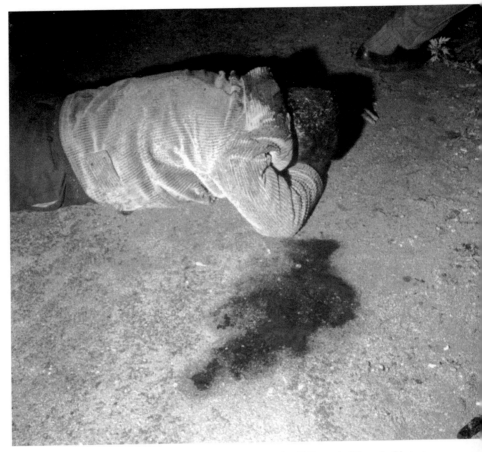

Paris, 17 October 1961: rue des Pâquerettes Nanterre
Death on the streets of Paris. Years later, an
official report admitted that many officers' batons
had been splintered by the force of the blows

Paris, 17 October 1961: Solferino metro station
A wounded demonstrator is led away as
fleeing protestors push their way past ❏

FRANK KERMODE

Palaces of memory

Whether it is a question of a single person, or a multitude of persons falsely represented by the self-biographer (selves-biographer?) as one, there is no avoiding the question of memory, as Augustine was the first to understand. We are warned that he used the term in a much wider sense than we do. For him it was the very instrument of personal continuity, the basis of self-identity, and 'the stomach of the mind' (*Confessions* X.8). And it was also the means of access to grace. Since his narrative is of a delayed self-opening to grace, memory is in every sense the basis of it.

Memory also offers the clue to the way the world at large functions, for the world is also fallen into materiality and sense, so that its redemption must be a matter of history, of a cosmic memory. One sees why Augustine follows his narrative with the philosophical enquiry into memory that occupies the tenth book of the *Confessions*. Here are some of the famous words:

> I come to the fields and vast palaces of memory, where are the treasuries of all kinds of objects brought in by sense perception. Hidden there is whatever we think about, a process which may increase or diminish or in some way alter the deliverance of the senses and whatever else has been deposited and placed on reserve and has not been swallowed up and buried in oblivion. When I am in this storehouse, I ask that it produce what I want to recall, and immediately certain things come out; some require a longer search, and have to be drawn out as it were from more recondite receptacles. Some memories pour out to crowd the mind, and when one is searching and asking for something quite different, leap forward into the centre as if saying, 'Surely we are what you want?' With the hand of my heart I chase them away from the face of my memory until what I want is freed of mist and emerges from its hiding places. Other memories come before me on demand with ease and without any confusion in their order. Memories of earlier events give way to those

which followed, and as they pass are stored away available for retrieval when I want them. And that is what happens when I recount a narrative from memory (X.viiii)

This is a simple model, basically rather like a library, and it does distinguish easy-access books from books on reserve. However, the books interact. What the senses have collected and stored is modified by association with 'whatever we think about'. Some items come easily, even too easily, so some must be waved away. Some are deep in the stacks or in special collections. The section that follows describes a sort of cataloguing system, in which acquisitions are organised according to the sense that introduced each of them: sight, sound, smell, taste, touch. Access to these resources enables one to enjoy and compare images of the world: 'I distinguish the odour of lilies from that of violets without smelling anything at all' (X.viii). And in these halls of memory 'I meet myself and recall what I am, what I have done, and when and where and how I was affected when I did it'; moreover, with those recollections other images less immediate to that self-meeting may in their turn be blended and combined.

To see what Augustine meant by self-exploration amid the contents of memory one needs to reflect that it is not merely sensory images that are collected and combined. Ideas are stored in the memory before one has learned them. As in Plato's *Meno*, though with the important difference that Augustine does not admit prenatal knowledge, learning is remembering. Similarly stored, part of the original deposit, are 'the affections of my mind'. Thus the rememberer can identify affective experiences when he or she has them later; but, as preserved in the memory and reported to the enquirer, they may differ strangely from what they were as primordial experience; and here the doubling effect is obvious: 'I can be far from glad in remembering myself to have been glad, and far from sad when I recall my past sadness. Without fear I remember how at a particular time I was afraid . . . I remember with joy a sadness that has passed and with sadness a lost joy' (X.xiv).

Forgetfulness in Augustine's *memoria* is treated as a fact of memory: 'memory retains forgetfulness . . . So it is there lest we forget what, when present, make us forget' (X.xv). I must remember forgetfulness, even though it destroys what I remember. One further point: how is it possible to aspire, as everybody does, to a felicity which, though we have the idea of it, we have never actually experienced? We have no memory,

in the ordinary sense of the word, of any earlier happiness on which
to model such hopes. Yet where else can they come from, if not from
memory? The notion of happiness must be there, put there by some
prior agency, innate. God, too, is in the memory, but by his own
intervention, to be found there perhaps very late, when fascination with
his creation gives way to love of him. Here comes the requirement of
continence, a degree of abnegation, achievable only by grace. *Da quod
iubes.* God must give the continence he commands. Only then will he
be found, and the enquiring spirit enabled to meet itself.

From this remarkable passage we can derive the idea of a necessary
doubleness, and also the notion that the experience as remembered is
not, affectively, of the same quality as the experience itself; or, as one
almost needs to say, the experience as remembered is not the same as
the experience remembered. Here is another aspect of difference in
doubleness. A pain recalled is recognised as a pain, yet it may be recalled
with pleasure; a past joy can be remembered with intense sadness (a
point perhaps remembered by Dante, in a famous passage, as well as
by Wordsworth). Augustine is sure, as many of his successors have been,
that what memory celebrates is not, in tone or significance, identical
with the actual moment remembered. For, as he remarks in Book
XI.xviii, meditating on past and future: 'the memory produces not the
actual events which have passed away but words conceived from images
of them, which they fixed in the mind like imprints as they passed
through the senses . . . when I am recollecting and telling my story, I
am looking on its image in present time . . .' This image belongs to what
he calls 'the present of things past'. Other memories have worked on the
image, and Augustine here anticipates the Freudian *Nachtraglichkeit*, or
deferred action (Freud spoke of 'memory-traces being subjected from
time to time to a rearrangement in accordance with fresh circumstances
– to a retranscription'). Forgetfulness affects memories, of course, but
memories can do the work of forgetfulness by modifying the original
deposit, which is further changed when the product of time and much
reworking must suffer a translation into language.

For Augustine any such translation must be a fall. Language, in
its nature successive, is part of the fallen world, the world of time. He
sets the word against the Word; the Word belongs to the simultaneous
present, the *nunc stans*, of eternity. In a famous passage (XI.xxviii)
Augustine speaks of reciting a psalm. Before he begins to do so he has

an expectation directed towards a whole. Verse by verse, as he recites, it passes into memory; so there is a blend of memory and expectation. But his attention is on the present, through which the future passes into the past. As he goes on, memory expands and expectation diminishes until the whole psalm has been said, and all is in the memory. The same action occurs in the life of the individual person, 'where all actions are parts of a whole, and also of the total history of the "sons of men" (Ps. 30:20) where all human lives are but parts'. So one's life, in this respect like all other lives, passes into memory and has a typical near-completeness which, so long as we remain alive, we can seek in the memory; always remembering that when we report it in words we have in some measure to undo that completeness, both because we are using words, and because memory always entails forgetting.

Sigmund Freud (1856–1939).
Credit: AKG London

Although he stresses certain dualisms in the action of memory, Augustine does not doubt the continuous individuality of the 'I' which is doing the remembering and the forgetting. Nevertheless, he sees his life, and the life of all the fallen, as a collection of scattered fragments. But he is far from wanting to represent the memory-image and his own report of it as such; for in achieving closure, totality, it has taken on a kind of intemporality, it imitates the eternal Word. His story is in fact of the unification of those fragments by his conversion, the terminus of his narrative, the conquest of division. So in this matter of fragmentation and dispersal of the self you could say he is aware of the problems of memory and subjectivity, but not that he would have recognised his problem as expressed in the language of Nietzsche or that he could have accepted the rhetorical and formal solutions offered by Roland Barthes or Paul Valéry in the *Cahiers*. Augustine recognises fragmentation but his whole drift is to mend it. He is thus antithetical to these writers, and also to Henry Adams, who expressly wanted to deny the illusion of unity in his life, to bring it back 'from unity to multiplicity'. This is the counter-Augustinian trend in modern autobiography. But the Augustinian strain remains strong.

Our modern assumptions about memory are likely to refer more directly to the Freudian tradition. In a recent paper called 'Freud and the Uses of Forgetting' the psychoanalyst Adam Phillips begins by remarking that 'People come for psychoanalytic treatment because they are remembering in a way that does not free them to forget.' Symptoms are involuntary and disguised memories of desire, unsuccessful attempts at self-cure. Those memories need to be forgotten, but desire, for Freud, is unforgettable. Repression is simply a way of seeming to get rid of things by keeping them. There is no cure for memory, though we try to use it to forget with, as in screen memories, devices designed to enable us to forget memories of a forbidden desire. Psychoanalysis attempts a cure by inducing the kind of remembering that makes forgetting possible. The only certain cure is death.

St Augustine. Ceiling fresco, Venice, by Nicoletto Semitecolo, 14th century. Credit: AKG London / Cameraphoto

Here are paradoxes on remembering and forgetting that represent the two as a doublet and in that respect are faintly reminiscent of Augustine's; but the differences are at least as marked. Phillips can think of the logic of Freud's psychoanalytical process as being the reverse of what we take to be the autobiographer's: 'Either the most significant bits of one's past are unconscious, and only available in the compromised form of symptoms and dreams; or the past is released through interpretation into oblivion.' Forgetting is the only way to remember; remembering is the only way to achieve benign forgetting. The product of analysis is not autobiography but evacuation. And Phillips finds in the analyst's ideal state of 'free-floating' or 'evenly suspended attention'

FRANK KERMODE

a parallel use of forgetting; the analyst must learn not to mind not having things in mind, he works by not trying to remember. This is not, to most people's way of thinking, at all like the practice of attentive reading (though it is sometimes held to be the correct practice, as in the writings of André Green and some others).

So the concept of memory offered by psychoanalysis is at first sight hostile to the truth of autobiography. What we profess to remember is what we have devised to protect us from the truth; and this will be the case even when, or perhaps especially when, the attempt to hide nothing is exceptionally strenuous and well advertised, as with Jean Jacques Rousseau. The concept of *Nachtraglichkeit* explains how a past is recovered in a distorted form; a childhood memory becomes a trauma, a trauma not directly associated with a 'real' childhood memory. Memory invents a past. Its reworkings defend us against the appalling timelessness of the unconscious. What we remember we may remember because we are forgetting in the wrong way; our remembering then takes the form of repetition, of acting out. If the analyst cures this repetition by fostering 'the work of remembering' he is not doing it because the memories thus elicited are valuable, but because he wants to dispose of them as bad for the patient, as what he needs to forget. 'Psychoanalysis is a cure by the kind of remembering that makes forgetting possible.'

Here the timeless is not, as in Augustine, eternity, but the unconscious, and we struggle against its forces, using substitute memories, writing about what ought to be disposed of precisely because of its inauthentic link to the unconscious. There are deposited anterior memories, and Augustine had those, but his were related to felicity and to God, not to incest and murder. Augustine needs access to the timeless, but our need is rather to forget it as totally as possible. We achieve access to its contents by the dual imaginative activity of the transference, but we do so with the object not of verifying them but of destroying them: to remember them, or even seem to do so, is a stratagem to relinquish or dispose of them. But Augustine needed them alive, because he sought the timeless for reasons having nothing to do with destruction; he wished to account for his life as a whole, given shape, made so by the action of memory and the timelessness into which it passes when it is finished.

There seems little doubt that the dominant myth of autobiography is still Augustinian rather than Freudian. Of course it may be that all autobiography is in Freudian terms defensive or resistant, that to totalise, to close, to advertise a psychic structure that cannot on a strict view be authentic, is false and evasive. But it seems to be true that what excites many writers is to achieve some measure or simulacrum of closure, and thus a substitute timelessness. Tolstoy got over being impressed by Rousseau's *Confessions* when he decided that, far from demonstrating the love of truth, Rousseau lied and believed his lies, which of course made him incapable of the truth to which he claimed to aspire. Rousseau himself admits that he left things out – from very pure motives – and occasionally made things up. Nabokov's artful autobiography is full of elegantly rendered and various detail, but, as he once remarks, what gives such a work its formal value is thematic repetition. John Sturrock is especially interested in the phenomenon, so often repeated in autobiography as to be endoxically recognisable, of what he calls the 'turn' – the point of epiphany or conversion, seen as the moment when the person under description individuates or selves himself, as it were, finds the point from which all can be seen to cohere, and so achieves a kind of closure. This moment is present in some form virtually everywhere. It draws on or constitutes the memory of a deviance, often apparently quite slight, from some norm of experience or behaviour, a deviance that makes the writer, in his own eyes at any rate, worth writing about as a single person. In the process he cannot avoid providing relevant material on what he takes himself to be deviating from, so that autobiography appeals to our notions of normality as well as to our interest in the myriad possible deviancies; and to our interest also in wholeness, a quality we seek when recounting to ourselves our own lives. Everybody takes these things for granted, and if they want confirmations they will look for their best expression not in the narratives of analysands, which require a different and specialised form of attention, but in the works of people who understand the conditions of art: say, in poets such as Wordsworth. For to communicate persuasively the experience of the turn it is necessary to practise an art.

Kinds of memory are subject to various sorts of classification, but we are familiar, largely on the evidence of works of art, with the idea that there is a rough, recognisable distinction between two kinds of memory, roughly voluntary and involuntary. Those 'turns', those hinges or fulcra on which a whole narrative depends and which justify the very existence of the narrative, are a very conspicuous, very 'placed', treatment of involuntary movements of consciousness momentarily present in some more accessible area of the memory, brought, as Augustine might have said, from special collections to open shelves, and then displayed against a background of simpler recollection. Now, their subtly fine bindings gleaming against the drab covers of commonplace recollections, they stand out, and seem worthwhile recounting. Though they are the sort of thing that can, perhaps does, occur to everybody, these privileged moments are not easy to put into words; they are not only what the author is really about but also a test of whether he ought to be an author.

I will borrow from Barrett J. Mandel a neat little illustration from Edmund Gosse's *Father and Son*. The author describes it as one of the many 'trifling things' that make up a life, but still 'a landmark'. The boy's fundamentalist father wanted him to decline an invitation to a party, and suggested that he pray for guidance from the Lord as to whether he should go. Asked what the Lord's answer was, the boy, well knowing his father's confidence that God's response would favour his own view, nevertheless replied, 'The Lord says I may go to the Browns.' The father 'gazed at me in speechless horror' and left the room, 'slamming the door'. Mandel admires this and calls it genuine autobiography, but adds that the writer Gosse knows more about the father and his thoughts than the boy Gosse can have done, and for that reason is able to pinpoint this moment as one of significant rebellion, a type of such resistance, and set it in a larger context that explains why it was significant, a landmark and not a trifle – or, perhaps better, despite its *seeming* a trifle, and getting called that by an author who wishes us to understand that he can now see how things hang together in a larger view of his remembered life. It is the mature, hindsighted record of an important stage in the widening gulf between father and son, part of a narrative designed to chart that process. We allow without demur that Gosse could not possibly be remembering his father's precise words; we already know, from our own memories, the nature of the relation of such a moment to truth and memory. As Mandel expresses it, the author is saying to the reader: 'My life was as this tale I am telling.' This is a satisfying formula, and it implies a claim that in this form (as this tale) it will have power to indicate landmarks and confer meaning on what would otherwise be mnemonic trifles.

We can add that an episode of this sort could have been worked over, told and retold to the author himself and perhaps to others; as the memory of a memory, of many memories perhaps, it acquires those associations of which Augustine speaks. To give this degree of centrality, of totality, to a memory, or to 'thematise' in the way recommended by Nabokov, is to seek to confer on the narrative a power to eliminate the restrictions of time; to institute its own laws of causality, to endow it with totality by invoking what WB Yeats called 'the artifice of eternity'. Much autobiography presumes to imitate that power.

Wordsworth offers an account of his life as 'this tale I am telling', though he might have accepted both the ultimate relation of time-dispersed elements to eternity, as adumbrated by Augustine, and the apparent triviality of some of the scattered episodes in themselves. Certain elements in this exercise in self-distinguishing are worth mention. Like Rousseau, Wordsworth is aware of the double consciousness all autobiographers must contend with. Childhood days have 'self-presence' in his mind (*The Prelude* ii.30–32); but more generally it is the present consciousness that speaks of a remote past recreated, remembered sometimes without his being able to give simple reasons for the memory. The most memorable of these memories, I suppose, are those spots of time: the gibbet, the girl with the pitcher, the bleak music of an old stone wall. These are the memories that count, and they count because the language that expresses their freight of emotion is, so to speak, adequately inadequate: it cannot verbalise what was not verbal, and so devotes itself to mystery and even discomfort.

There are other escapes; one of the great things about Wordsworth, as with Augustine, is that one sees them as constituents of that calm society he could, at the end of this story, with pained rejoicing, detect in himself. For loss, and these insistent premonitions of further loss, he needs consolation, a word that occurs, in company with a 'strength' that endures, as early as *The Prelude* iii.108 (1805). Yet the fulcrum, the moment of illumination, comes a little later, when, after a night of dancing, he moves through 'a common dawn' and recognises, although making no vows, that nevertheless 'vows were then made for me'; that henceforth he would be, 'else sinning greatly, / A dedicated spirit. On I walked / In blessedness, which even yet remains' (*The Prelude* iv.337–45).

The *kind* of experience, here so delicately rendered, recurs in most autobiographies, always as a claim to distinction, to the stigma of individuality, of election, though as a rule far less distinguished. For in the end what distinguishes is not the experience itself but the force and authority of the language claiming it. The religious tone is unmistakable, the sense of involuntary vocation calmly accepted; the boldness and pathos of that 'even yet remains'. It is, we say, pure Wordsworth.

The Prelude is the greatest and most original of English autobiographies, but it is so not because Wordsworth's intention is so different from most others. What we see particularly clearly in his prose is his desire to break through the assumptions and habits controlling or limiting normal introspection, as they limit poetry. The forces that break through, and enable deeper self-examination, are all anterior in origin to the formation of customary and habitual behaviour, shades of the prison-house; they are deep in the memory and hard to reach because of the distracting mist and clamour of ordinary life. But the memory, for a time at any rate, is accessible, its records can be reached, brought up from the deep store. It is not surprising that Wordsworth used the Platonic trope of anamnesis, for, as Augustine also knew, the memory contains what seems not to have been put into it by the senses. Probably many vocations are discovered by some such process. These deep, vertiginous mnemonic plunges most of us know about from literature rather than from ourselves – not because we are denied them, but because they have to be given appropriate expression or enactment. The question as to what sorts of people are capable of doing this – what sorts of people should be writing autobiography anyway – I must, for the moment, leave unanswered. ❏

Frank Kermode*'s autobiography* Not Entitled *was reprinted in paperback in 1997 (Flamingo). His latest book is* Shakespeare's Language *(Penguin, 2000)*

FLASHPOINT

The Empire closes in

A series of linked incidents is raising concern for press freedom in China-ruled Hong Kong. On 20 October, the Broadcasting Authority released a draft code of conduct. This will require all presenters of radio commentary programmes to declare any commercial interests, and for audiences to be reminded every 30 minutes that any views expressed are those of the individual host. The Hong Kong Journalists' Association (HKJA) said: 'It would appear that the Broadcasting Authority is attempting to turn itself from regulator to editor.'

Zhao Qichen, minister of the State Council's Information Office, and Guo Shuyang, director of the State Council's Three Gorges [Dam] Project Committee, condemned Hong Kong's *South China Morning Post* (*SCMP*) on 26 October for 'inaccuracies and exaggerations' in its reports of corruption surrounding the vast dam project, and for questioning the dam's ultimate viability. Zhao said: 'We think the inaccuracy ratio of *SCMP*'s China coverage is very high.'

A new 'anti-stalking' law in Hong Kong might, suggested the HKJA on 31 October, restrict the legitimate activities of reporters. The argument hangs on a distinction between 'reasonable' and 'unreasonable' conduct in gathering news, and whether a journalist's activities would cause 'alarm and distress'. The HKJA proposed that a provision be included for the defence of 'acting in the public interest': it pointed out that any individual under justified media scrutiny would, indeed, feel distress, and could therefore seek an injunction under the new law. The Law Reform Commission rejected the proposal.

The *SCMP* was at the centre of another furore on 4 November when Willy Wo Lap Lam resigned as the paper's veteran China editor, pre-empting his removal from the desk as part of 'organisational changes' at the paper. Lam claimed in an interview on 8 November that Robert Keatley, *SCMP*'s editor-in-chief, had demanded to vet his work for 'politically incorrect material'. This had been the case since June when he first reported Beijing officials had pressed a meeting of Hong Kong

Simon Davies on

PRIVACY

Ursula Owen on

HATE SPEECH

Patricia Williams on

RACE

Gabriel Garcia Marquez on

JOURNALISM

John Naughton on

THE INTERNET

... all in   INDEX

tycoons – including *SCMP*'s proprietors – to show stronger support for embattled Hong Kong Chief Executive Tung Chee-hwa, in return for favourable treatment.

SCMP's main shareholder, Robert Kuok Hock Nien, published an angry refutation, accusing Lam of 'distortions and speculation', but Lam's version is supported by others who were present at the meeting. 'There are genuine fears from me and among other colleagues . . . that there are increasing attempts to de-politicise the China coverage, to steer it away from sensitive political matters,' said Lam, who suggested the restructuring plan was a 'trick' to get rid of 'troublesome employees'. 'Beijing is extremely sensitive towards the Hong Kong media,' he said, 'so it is possible they have put pressure on other news media to rein in the reporting of a number of journalists.'

Proposals unveiled on 7 November to modify the Police General Order in Hong Kong could ban officers from talking to the media in a private capacity without the consent of their superiors. Officers would also need to ensure that any comments to the press on matters unrelated to their work could not be misinterpreted as representing the views of the force. Officers' associations say the proposals would breach provisions for freedom of expression under the Basic Law and the Bill of Rights.

Following President Jiang Zemin's furious outburst against Hong Kong reporters in October (see p10), eight reporters and a cable TV crew from Hong Kong were detained by police for three hours on 14 November and prevented from covering a ceremony in Shenzhen where Jiang and Tung were unveiling a statue of Deng Xiaoping. Shenzhen officials claim the venue was 'too small' to accommodate Hong Kong's press, though they had attended a similar event ten years previously. They were released 45 minutes after Jiang had left the area.

And on 15 November, during a meeting about Hong Kong and international affairs, President Jiang announced he would 'take the lead not to read [Hong Kong's *Apple Daily*] and set an example.' The paper has been a consistent critic of Beijing. After his remarks, government offices cancelled their subscriptions. 'How could we have such an honour to be blacklisted?' mused the proprietor, Jimmy Lai Chee-ying. 'I didn't think we were powerful enough to get such attention.' ❏

Ben Carddus

A *censorship chronicle incorporating information from the American Association for the Advancement of Science Human Rights Action Network (AAASHRAN), Amnesty International (AI), Article 19 (A19), Alliance of Independent Journalists (AJI), the BBC Monitoring Service Summary of World Broadcasts (SWB), Centre for Journalism in Extreme Situations (CJES), the Committee to Protect Journalists (CPJ), Canadian Journalists for Free Expression (CJFE), Glasnost Defence Foundation (GDF), Information Centre of Human Rights & Democracy Movements in China (ICHRDMC), Instituto de Prensa y Sociedad (IPYS), The UN's Integrated Regional Information Network (IRIN), the Inter-American Press Association (IAPA), the International Federation of Journalists (IFJ/FIP), Human Rights Watch (HRW), the Media Institute of Southern Africa (MISA), Network for the Defence of Independent Media in Africa (NDIMA), International PEN (PEN), Open Media Research Institute (OMRI), Pacific Islands News Association (PINA), Radio Free Europe/ Radio Liberty (RFE/RL), Reporters Sans Frontières (RSF), the World Association of Community Broadcasters (AMARC), World Association of Newspapers (WAN), the World Organisation Against Torture (OMCT) and other sources*

ANGOLA

On 31 October **Rafael Marques**, **Gustavo Costa** and **Aguiar dos Santos** were given suspended sentences for articles published in the weekly independent *Agora* in July 1999 (*Index* 2/2000,

3/2000, 5/2000, 6/2000). A condition attached to Marques's sentence is that he not speak in public, practise journalism or leave the country for five years. If he violates any of these conditions, he is liable to serve two to eight months in prison. (MISA)

On 9 November the home of journalist **Isidoro Natalicio** was picketed by demonstrators claiming to be war veterans. Natalicio said the demonstration was orchestrated by the governor of Kwanza-Norte whom he had accused of failing to pay public-sector workers. (MISA)

ARGENTINA

Rubén Viejo, a reporter with FM Ciudad in the Pico Truncado region of Santa Cruz province, received a death threat on 1 October. An unidentified individual put a gun to his head and warned him that if he did not stop his investigation into the recent murder of a taxi driver either he or his family would be assassinated. (IFJ)

On 20 November **Eduardo Delbono**, owner of and reporter for radio station Ciudad de Merlo, received a death threat from two individuals while driving his van through the Ituzaingo region of Buenos Aires. One man threatened his life if his involvement with the municipality did not cease. Delbono claims that his persecution started after he refused to comply with a Merlo district directive that banned statements broadcast by local citizens criticising the Merlo administration. (Periodistas)

ARMENIA

On 30 October four TV companies – Armenia A1+, Ar, Russian ORT and Noyan Tapan – had videotapes confiscated which documented how dozens of plain-clothes policemen had smashed through the door of Arkadi Vardanian's office and arrested him. Vardanian, a politician and president of the independent association 21 Century, was due to attend a political meeting when the incident occurred. A reporter with Armenia A1+, **Mher Arshakian**, who witnessed the arrest and had recorded the events on video, was detained for two and a half hours. (RFE/RE, IWPR)

AUSTRIA

Professor **Anton Pelinka** was acquitted on 25 October of a charge of defamation brought against him by Jörg Haider (*Index* 4/2000). Political analyst Pelinka had compared some of Haider's words to Nazi propaganda. (*Daily Telegraph, International Herald Tribune*)

AZERBAIJAN

The tax department of Khatainski district of Baku City undertook an audit of independent newspaper *Avropa* in October. After a prolonged search it revealed no financial violations, but bowed to administrative pressure and fined *Avropa* US$3,700. Editor **Fakhry Ugurlu** said that prior to this incident the paper had been fined the maximum amount in a legal suit brought under false pretences. (CPJ)

After the closure of independent TV station ABA on 3 October, the station's president, **Faik Zulfugarov**, announced that he would sue state officials. ABA had paid off its debt of one billion manat (US$300,000) but transmissions and the legitimate rights of the company have not been restored (*Index* 6/2000). (IFJ)

BAHRAIN

Jassem Hussein Ali, a senior lecturer in business administration at Bahrain University and Manama-based contributor to *The Economist*, was released on 10 November after being detained for ten days. No reason was given for his arrest but he was reportedly questioned over his work for *The Economist* Intelligence Unit. (WAN, Digital Freedom Network)

BANGLADESH

On 20 October a group of ruling Awami League youth activists assaulted **Sohrab Hossain**, a reporter with the regional Bengali-language daily *Loksamaj*, after he wrote an article critical of the government's flood relief efforts. (Media Watch, CPJ, RSF)
State Minister for Social Welfare Mozammel Hossain ordered Awami League members and local bureaucrats on 25 October to 'break' the bones of journalists wherever they came across them. Hossain gave the order in Satkhira, a town that had recently experienced terrible flooding. (Media Watch, CPJ, RSF)

On 26 October a mob led by local Awami League leader Asadul Haq ransacked the offices of the local daily *Satkhirar Chitro*, and assaulted **Anisur Rahim**, the paper's editor. The attack followed the newspaper's reporting on the misappropriation of disaster relief funds following the recent flooding. (Media Watch, CPJ, RSF, WAN)
Monwar Islam, a reporter for the daily tabloid *Manavjamin* and Secretary General of the Dhaka Reporters Unity, escaped a kidnapping attempt on 27 October. Two armed men tried to get Islam into their car, but were scared off by passers-by. (Media Watch)
On 6 November the Working Committee of the Awami League met to decide how to react to the daily *Inqilab*'s publication on 20 October of a parody of the national anthem that mocked the administration of Prime Minister Sheik Hasina. Within days of the meeting, Awami League leaders filed treason charges against *Inqilab* in six separate courts. On 13 November, the Home Ministry filed its own complaint, accusing **AMM Bahauddin**, Inqilab's editor; **ASM Baki Billah**, the publisher; and **AS Mosharraf**, the author of the parody, with sedition. Arrest warrants were also issued that day, and the police used them immediately to raid the Dhaka offices of *Inqilab*, as well as the homes of Bahauddin and Baki Billah. No one was arrested but **M Mainuddin**, the director of the Inqilab Group and the brother of Bahauddin and Baki Billah, was arrested on 14 November under the draconian Special Powers Act.

Meanwhile, on 20 November, Abdul Hasnat Abdullah, an Awami League official in Barisal, announced that *Inqilab* was banned in the southern region. (CPJ)
On 30 November Pakistan recalled Irfanur Raja, its deputy high commissioner, from Dhaka three days after Raja had alleged that the ruling Awami League - and not the Pakistani army - was responsible for starting atrocities in Bangladesh's 1971 war for independence. (BBC News Online)
Recent Publication: *Torture and impunity (AI, November 2000, pp32)*

BELARUS

The editor-in-chief of the Vitebsk-based independent newspaper *Vybar* (Choice), **Boris Khamaida**, was summoned by the financial police on 25 October to hear a proposal to close down the newspaper. (Radio Racjyja)
The Soros Foundation is suing the government following its 16 October seizure of Soros-owned printing equipment at the Minsk publishing house Magic. According to the government, the Soros Foundation, which ceased activity in Belarus several years ago, still owes the government US$78,000 and the seizure was to offset this debt. Magic prints most of the country's independent and opposition periodicals including *Narodnaya Volya*, *Rabochy* (*Index* 6/2000) and *Nasha Svaboda*. (CJES)
The computers, printers, scanners and production equipment of the largest independent regional daily, *Shag*, were stolen on 16 November,

when its offices in Baranovichi were broken into and robbed by armed men. (WAN)

A number of media outlets have received emails from an address on the yahoo.com free server which accuse President Aleksandr Lukashenko's Security Service of killing Russian Public Television cameraman **Dmitry Zavadski** and opposition politician **Viktar Hancher**, who disappeared in September 1999. The sender identified himself as a Belarusan KGB officer and claimed that the KGB arrested nine people, including five officers of the presidential security services who confessed to killing Zavadski and burying him near Minsk. (RFE/RL)

BOLIVIA

A gag law or *ley mordaza* has been definitively prevented from going through the National Congress as a result of protests and demonstrations by professional and labour organisations and the media. The bill sought to annul the 1925 Press Law which guarantees freedom of press by stipulating that a pluralist jury should review press crimes. (IAPA)

BRITAIN

Figures released by the Commissioner, Lord Nolan, have shown that the 2,022 warrants issued for phone-tapping and mail-opening were the second highest since records began. The figures, however, do not include warrants issued by MI5, MI6, GCHQ and the RUC. (Statewatch)

Recently empowered by the Local Government Act to set its own rules, the Welsh Assembly is contemplating a ban on reporters covering Cabinet meetings in Welsh councils, it was reported on 13 October. Press and public alike could be excluded whenever it was felt that they would be likely to 'inhibit the free and frank exchange of views for the purposes of deliberation'. (*Press Gazette*)

The much-criticised RIP Act came into effect on 24 October. The Lawful Business Practice regulations came into power on the same day, giving businesses the right to read employees' emails and monitor their Internet use. These regulations sit uneasily alongside the guidelines of the Data Commissioner on employee privacy, which protect the right of the employee to private and unmonitored communications. The regulations are also contradicted in Article 8 of the new Human Rights Act which ensures the individual's right to privacy. (*Daily Telegraph*)

Prosecutors dropped charges on 1 November against retired army officer Lieutenant-Colonel **Nigel Wylde**, who stood accused of passing information to journalist **Tony Geraghty** about surveillance operations in Northern Ireland (*Index* 2/1999, 2/2000, 4/2000, 5/2000, 6/2000). Freelance journalist **Duncan Campbell** (*Index* 5/1998), as an expert witness to the defence, showed that all the material Wylde was accused of passing was already in the public domain. (*Guardian*)

Punch magazine and its editor, **James Steen**, were fined £25,000 by the High Court on 7 November for publishing an article by former MI5 officer **David Shayler**. The article breached an injunction imposed in 1997 since it contained material about the 1993 Bishopsgate bombing in London. Soon after, Steen left *Punch*, citing the case as a contributory factor in his resignation. (*Daily Telegraph, Guardian, Press Gazette*).

Cabinet Office Minister Lord Falconer tried to censor an 'official history' of the Millennium Dome in November 1999, it was reported on 8 November. In a recently leaked letter written to the ex-chief executive of the failed attraction, Jennie Page, Falconer stated that the government would not agree to the publication of *Regeneration: The Story of the Dome* by **Adam Nicolson**, unless 'certain amendments' were made. Falconer justified his intervention as an exercise in correcting inaccuracies. It has since emerged, however, that most of these so-called inaccuracies were true. (*The Times*)

On 13 November Cherie Booth, wife of the prime minister, obtained an injunction in the High Court against **Nel Lister**, a friend of their former nanny **Ros Mark**. A confidentiality agreement signed when Mark was first employed forbade her from disclosing any information about the family; her friend Lister is prevented by the new injunction from revealing what Mark had told her about her experiences. The judge ordered Lister to hand over three computer disks containing material from Mark, and to pay £15,000

in costs. (*Guardian*, *Daily Telegraph*)
The inquiry into the 1972 Bloody Sunday massacre resumed on 13 November. Hundreds of soldiers are arguing that their safety was compromised by the disclosure of their identities, and that they should not have to give evidence in Londonderry. Although the decision of the chairman of the inquiry, Lord Saville of Newdigate, to disclose their names was overturned by the courts, the men are worried that their faces can be linked with previously leaked details. (*The Times*)
It was revealed on 30 November that an army whistleblower, known under the pseudonym **Martin Ingram**, will not be prosecuted for breaking the Official Secrets Act as was feared. Ingram was charged following his revelation of information about Force Research Unit collusion with military intelligence in a series of articles in the *Sunday Times*. (*Guardian*)

BULGARIA

On 2 November Justice Minister Teodossyi Simeonov hit an 18-year-old photographer working for Sega newspaper. The minister, one of the least popular in the government, cited his constitutional right not to be photographed without permission as an excuse for hitting the photographer. (GHM)

BURKINA FASO

On 19 August three members of the presidential guard were found guilty of confining and torturing **David Ouedrago**,

the chauffeur of the president's brother, Francis Compaore. Two were sentenced to 20 years' imprisonment while the third received ten. As yet no one has been charged with the 1998 assassination of **Norbert Zongo**, a journalist for *L'Indépendent*, who had concluded that Francis Compaore had been involved in Ouedrago's killing. (*Index* 4/1999, 5/1999, 6/1999, 1/2000, 4/2000). (RSF)

BURMA

James Mawdsley (*Index* 6/1999, 1/2000, 6/2000) was freed from Insein Prison on 20 October. Although he was allegedly released because of international pressure, the military regime claimed it was 'a charitable gesture'. (*Guardian*)
As of 16 October, reports say that journalist Soe Thein is dying. Jailed in May 1996 for writing on 'peaceful resistance', he fell ill in September after a suspected heart attack. Denied trial under Article 10 of the State Protection Law, he was also imprisoned in 1990 for publishing the magazine *Ah-Twe-Ah-Mye* (The Thought). (RSF)

CANADA

On 1 November the Superior Court of Justice in Toronto ruled that police could keep the footage they seized from eight television stations and newspapers of an anti-poverty protest in Ontario. It was reported on 9 November that Mr Justice Frank Roberts had permitted the police to use the material to further their investigations. However, the

footage will remain sealed until the media outlets have decided whether to appeal. (CJFE)

CHAD

On 9 November the jounalist and retired public servant **Garonde Djarama** was arrested and charged with defamation. Two days earlier, Djarama had published an article in the daily *N'Djaména Hebdo*, in which he criticised the authorities' inadequate reaction to racist attacks against Chadian nationals in Libya. The director of *N'Djaména Hebdo*, **Oulatar Begoto Nicolas**, was also summoned by the Criminal Investigation Department and interrogated. (RSF)

CHINA

Falun Gong adherents continue to fall foul of the authorities in numbers too great to record here in detail. For fully referenced information about victims of the persecution from 7 October to 7 December, please visit: www.indexoncensorship.org/news/
Yang Xiaofeng, editor of the *Lanzhou Daily* and *Lanzhou Evening News* in Gansu Province, was demoted and two other journalists were dismissed in September for 'breaking news discipline'. Yang had dispatched the journalists to cover a large explosion on 8 September in Urumqi, the capital of Xinjiang Province, in which 73 people died and 300 were injured. The stories and pictures were published and picked up by other papers

before the official Xinhua news agency had published a version of the incident, because of concerns that the explosion was a terrorist attack by Muslim separatists. Xinhua reserves the authority to interpret and release all major news stories before other media. (Agence France-Presse, Reuters, RSF)

Beijing reacted angrily to the award of the Nobel Prize for Literature to the Paris-based exiled writer **Gao Xingjian**, whose work is banned in China. A statement from the Foreign Ministry on 12 October said that the award 'shows again that the Nobel Literature Prize has been used for ulterior political motives, and is not worth commenting on'. (Agence France-Presse, Hong Kong iMail)

Xinhua reported ten people were sentenced to prison on 2 November in Guangzhou on charges of illegally printing and selling books. The harshest sentences were passed on **Liang Jiantian**, who was given life, and **Liu Jingsong**, who received 20 years, for publishing books about the Falun Gong movement. Two others had produced books about China's intelligence community. **Chen Weicheng**, **Xie Ri'an**, **Liu Lixin** and **Long Zhirong** were sentenced to 14, 11, seven and five years respectively. **Liu Yong**, among whose many publications was one he compiled about film stars, was sentenced to 15 years. (Xinhua)

A conference of 200 poets organised for 6–11 November by the Communist Youth League in Beihai, Guangxi Province, was banned and the organisers arrested when offi-

cials discovered known dissident writers had been invited to attend. **Wei Manzeng**, **Jiang Nan** and **Wang Chenghuai** were arrested on 4 November for organising the 'illegal assembly' and held in Beihai jail. Police were particularly aggrieved about the invitation of **Zhang Dao**, who has published work critical of the government on the Internet, and **Yang Chunguang**, who was arrested for activities during the 1989 democracy protests. (Reuters)

Beijing published a set of draft regulations in the *People's Daily* on 7 November, aimed at curtailing nine loosely defined 'web crimes', including anything that threatens 'state security', spreads 'feudal superstition' or which 'harms China's honour and interests'. All websites carrying news in China can now only publish material credited from official sources, although the term 'news' is not thought to include sport and entertainment. News sites must acquire special permission from the State Council Information Office if they want to include links to foreign news organisations, and must employ a team of 'experienced' editors – namely editors who have previously worked in the official media. The regulations state: 'No organisation or individual may develop bulletin board services without obtaining specific approval, or completing specific recording procedures.' (*People's Daily*)

A survivor of the 1937 Rape of Nanjing, Ms **Xia Shuqin**, 71, filed a libel suit on 28 November against two Japanese writers who claim that Ms Xia's testimony of the

massacre is false. Higashinakano Osamu and Magsumura Goshio also claim in their books, *Thorough Review of Nanjing Massacre* and *Big Question in Nanjing Massacre*, that all historical data about the massacre are not true. The case is significant as it is the first to be filed against people not held directly responsible for the massacre, but against people of a right-wing nationalist tendency in Japan who deny the wartime atrocities. (Hong Kong iMail, Reuters, Xinhua)

COLOMBIA

Journalist **Juan Camilo Restrepo Guerra**, head of community radio station Galaxia Estereo in northwestern Colombia, was shot dead on 31 October by a suspected right-wing paramilitary gunman. The killer allegedly arranged to meet Restrepo and shot him five times. It is thought that the 26-year-old was murdered for his coverage of local corruption. (IAPA, SIP)

TV journalist **Carlos Armando Uribe** and producer **Jorge Otalora** were kidnapped on 2 November by members of the ELN guerrilla force. Uribe and Otalora were filming the latest instalment of a weekly series for the National Coffee Growers' Federation (FNC) in Tolima province, when they were seized at gunpoint by seven plain-clothes guerrillas. Uribe, who is also a newspaper columnist and radio host, was released on 9 November. The guerrillas have threatened to hold the 60-year-old Otalora until the government and FNC pledge money for road improvements in northern Tolima. (CPJ)

Freelance radio journalist **Gustavo Rafael Ruiz Cantillo** was killed on 15 November by two unidentified gunmen in Pivijay. His former colleagues at local radio station Radio Galeon believe Ruiz was shot by members of a paramilitary group thought to be separate from the umbrella AUC. The paramilitaries had apparently threatened Ruiz twice before about giving 'negative' coverage to Pivijay province. (IAPA, SIP)

In a landmark ruling on 24 November a criminal court sentenced a man to 60 years in prison for the murder of two journalists three years earlier. Juan Carlos González Jaramillo was convicted for the death in May 1997 of **Mario Calderón** and **Elsa Alvarado**, both investigative journalists for the Research and Popular Education Centre (CINEP) (*Index* 4/1997). Two other men were sentenced. (IFJ)

Authorities have arrested three suspects for the attempted murder in June of **Eduardo Pilonieta**, a columnist for daily *Vanguardia Liberal* (*Index* 5/1999). Former union leader Jorge Humberto Torres Monsalve was detained on 24 November as the suspected intellectual author of the crime. Three days later, Fernando Maldonado Ortiz and Carlos Arturo Castillo were arrested as the alleged perpetrators. The attorney in charge of the case said that more arrests are likely. (IPYS)

CÔTE D'IVOIRE

Between General Robert Gueï's coup d'état in December 1999 and his overthrow in the general election of 22 October, 16 journalists and other media figures were arrested, seven were attacked and beaten by soldiers and six editorial offices were ransacked. No investigations have been made into any of the incidents. (RSF).

The racist feelings stirred up by ex-president Gueï are being upheld by the country's new leader, President Laurent Gbagbo. Several newspapers have fuelled these sentiments by referring to Gbagbo's rival **Alassane Ouattara** as a member of a 'cursed race' – the Burkinabés. *Le National* called Ouattara an 'American Negro' and his wife a 'white Jew'. The opposition Rassemblement des Démocrates Républicains (RDR) daily *Le Patriote* expressed anger at the repression of pro-Ouattara demonstrations and called for a new ballot. (RSF, *Courrier International*)

On 26 October **Bakary Nimaga**, editor-in-chief of *Le Libéral*, was arrested and beaten before being released several hours later. He was accused of spying for the RDR. On 27 October the offices of *Le Libéral* and another pro-RDR newspaper, *La Référence*, were ransacked by students. A curfew and state of emergency were extended until 28 October. (*West Africa*, RSF, AI)

CUBA

On 6 November **Luís Alberto Rivera Leyva**, director of Santiago de Cuba-based news agency Eastern Free Press, was summoned by the state security department and accused of defamation. He was told that this charge would be dropped if he abandoned his work for the independent press. (RSF)

On 9 November, the state security department searched the home of independent journalist **Rodríguez Saludes**, director of the New Press Agency. He was driven to the Sixth Unit of the National Police and then to the state security department where he was released later that evening. (RSF)

State security police took the director of the independent José María Rodríguez Library, **Zocima Simoneau Vidal**, into questioning on 7 November. The session was taped and, before her release, she was warned that she could be charged with 'defamation'. More than 60 uncensored libraries have opened across Cuba. (CubaNet)

State security forces blocked the surrounding streets and banned public access to the António Maceo Grajeles Library that was due to hold a seminar for a non-governmental teachers' organisation on 9 November. That evening in a nearby street an unidentified man accosted and threatened the director of the library, **Marcia Peréz Castillo**. She was warned against her 'counter-revolutionary activities'. (CubaNet)

An agent of the Department of State Security called *Independent* journalist **María Elena Rodrigues** to a meeting at the national identity card office on 14 November. She was accused of falsifying news and for being 'manipulated by the US'. She was questioned for four hours and threatened with

Law 88, passed last year to restrict freedom of the press. (CubaNet)

DEMOCRATIC REPUBLIC OF CONGO

André Tshowa Kabila, an activist with Journaliste en Danger, was arrested by soldiers on 17 October, stripped naked and subjected to a mock execution after they accused him of damaging his country's reputation. At the time of his arrest he was distributing a report entitled *Vers une nouvelle strategie pour la liberté d'expression*. (Journaliste en Danger)
Jean-Marie Basa Ndjanko, a journalist with the thrice-weekly Kinshasa newspaper *L'Alarme*, was arrested on 17 October by a group of Congolese Armed Forces (FAC) soldiers and accused of 'exposing military secrets'. *L'Alarme* had previously published an apparently positive view of improved security in several districts of Kinshasa. However, the journalist also touched on the techniques used to fight crime. He was imprisoned in the Kokolo military base and released on 24 October, after being beaten on a daily basis. (Journaliste en Danger)
Muboyayi Mubanga, **Alexis Mutanda** and **Zacharie Nyembo Kalenga**, publishers of the dailies *Le Potentiel*, *Le Phare* and *La Tempête des Tropiques*, and the weekly *Le Tribune*, were summoned to the offices of the Congolese National Police Special Services (SSP) in Kinshasa/Gombe on 16 October. The papers were accused of

publishing material that would demoralise the army and civilian population. All publications had in the previous week reported on rebel activity in the Mbandaka region, currently under government control. (Journaliste en Danger)
Subject to a 24 October decree, Minister of Communications Inongo has authorised Radio Sentinelle to broadcast anew. Since the station is owned by the independent Cité Bethél Church, it only broadcasts religious programmes. (Journaliste en Danger)
Rapid Intervention Police officers barred RTKM journalists from entering the station's studios and newsroom on 29 October. The formerly private-owned station was recently nationalised by order of Minister of Communications (*Index* 5/2000, 6/2000). A short time earlier on 28 October, RTKM programmes were abruptly interrupted by order of Victor Kasonga Mbunga, previously nicknamed 'Black Scissors' when he headed state-owned OZRT. (Journaliste en Danger)
Shimba Ndala has been forced to go underground after being actively sought by the National Information Agency. The publisher of the weekly newspaper *La Cheminée* in Lumbumbashi published an article about the search and sealing-off of the National Assembly's seat in Lubumbashi on 14 October. (Journaliste en Danger)
Feu d'Or Donsange Ifonge, **Arisote Dola**, **Kala Bokango** and **Guy Batshika**, journalists with *L'Alarme*, were

arrested on 11 November at the Place Victoire in Kinshasa/Kalamu while distributing issue 236 of their newspaper, published on that same day. Ifonge is said to be imprisoned and has been denied the right to food or visitations. (Journaliste en Danger)

EGYPT

A massive pre-election clampdown on the banned Muslim Brotherhood (MB) organisation resulted in the detention of up to 1,000 of the group's members in the run-up to the 14 November parliamentary elections. Supporters were turned away from polling stations, where members bypassed the banning order by standing as independent candidates, and were subjected to police intimidation. (*Cairo Times*, *Daily Telegraph*)
Associated Press reporter **Mariam Fam** was assaulted by a police officer on 24 October while covering elections in Ashmun. Fam had travelled to the northern town to question the authorities and voters about alleged malpractice. On arrival, she was challenged by police officers, one of whom punched her in the face and set about kicking her while she lay on the ground. (RSF, CNN)
On 26 October Minister of Information Safwat Al Sherif threatened to ban the Qatar-based satellite station Al Jazeera. Since it started broadcasting six months ago, Al Jazeera has attacked President Mubarak for 'betraying the *intifada*' by hosting peace talks between Israeli and Palestinian representatives. (*Cairo Times*)
The Egyptian Musicians

Syndicate announced on 2 November that any member who worked for Al Jazeera TV would be instantly dismissed from the organisation. (*Cairo Times*)

A fracas outside a polling station in Dokki, Cairo, where an MB leader was standing as candidate, descended into violence on 8 November when reporters challenged policemen who were seen denying people access to voting booths. Uniformed and plain-clothes officers beat Al Jazeera cameraman **Hossam Abou al-Magd** with a metal rod and smashed his camera. **Abeer Allam** and **Norbert Chiller**, respectively reporter and photographer for the *New York Times*, were assaulted by policemen, and **Dale Gavlak**, correspondent for Radio Vatican, had recording equipment seized. (RSF, WAN)

Attacks on journalists continued on 14 November when Agence France-Presse photographer **Marwan Naamani** was dragged from his car and beaten by a group of men claiming to be police informants. A few hours later, Associated Press correspondent **Sarah al-Dib** was thrown to the ground by two women, who then made off with her mobile phone and handbag, while reporting on the elections in the Bassatine district. The BBC's **Jehan Al Aleili** was surrounded by a crowd in the Al Weili district and was forced to relinquish her tape recorder. (RSF, *Cairo Times*)

Carsten Jurgensen, an Amnesty International delegate, was punched and kicked by policemen on 14 November while investigating reports of clashes between security forces and civilians in the province of Azbat Uthman. Jurgensen was accosted by plain-clothes officers who attempted to confiscate his camera and personal papers. The film from the camera was destroyed. (Egyptian Organisation for Human Rights)

Mohammed Abu Lawaya, a journalist with the now-defunct *Al Shabab* newspaper, was found guilty on 18 November of libelling the head of the Egyptian Journalists' Syndicate, Ibrahim Nafie. He was sentenced to six months' imprisonment by the Cairo court and ordered to pay a fine of US$2,000. The writer had distributed leaflets accusing Nafie of corruption. (*Cairo Times*)

ETHIOPIA

Tegenge, the editor-in-chief of private newspaper *Remet*, was initially detained in Addis Ababa for eight months on press violation charges and released on bail. On 9 October the court sentenced him to two months in prison, but closed the file since Tegenge had already served more than his time. (EFJA)

Eight journalists were detained for reporting on the war with Eritrea on 14 October. Six were released four days later but **Milkihas Mihretab**, editor of the private Tigrigna-language weekly *Keste Debena*, and **Yusuf Mohamed Ali**, from the weekly *Tsigenay*, are still detained in prison near Asmara for publishing 'unpatriotic information'. (WAN)

Taye Belachew, former editor-in-chief of the private Amharic monthly *Tobia*, was fined US$1,500 on 17 October for 'disseminating false news' and 'arousing hatred against Tigrigna-speaking people'. Belachew was held for 72 days in connection with the incident. (EFJA)

Tewdoros Kassa, former editor-in-chief of *Ethiop* newspaper, faces a fine of US$1,800 in addition to one year in prison for 'fabricating evidence in a newspaper that could incite people to political violence', it was reported on 15 November. Kassa has already served his prison term for writing an article which suggested that the state security apparatus had killed **Duki Feyssa**, a member of the Oromo Liberation Front. He is prepared to fight his case on the second charge. (EFJA)

The current editor-in-chief of *Ethiop*, **Meles Shine**, appeared in court on 15 November for an article entitled 'Eritrean opposition forces are receiving training in areas of Rama and Assayita'. Shine is expected to remain in prison for two years while awaiting trial. (EFJA)

The former editor-in-chief of *Atkurot*, **Zemedkun Moges**, was released from prison on 17 November. First imprisoned for two years in December 1997 (*Index* 1/2000), a further charge of disseminating false information was brought against him in March 1999. (EFJA)

Vice-president of EFJA **Zegeye Haile**, who is also publisher of the newspaper *Genanaw*, was arrested on 23 November by the Central Investigations Department (CID). During the past week, editors-in-chief of three newspapers have been released after making statements to the CID. The papers were *Gohe*, *Abissinya* and *Mahlet*. (EFJA)

FIJI

It was reported on 23 October that Fiji Television was warned by acting Information Minister Ratu Inoke Kubuabola not to feature deposed prime minister **Mahendra Chaudry** on its flagship current affairs programme *Close Up*, on the grounds that an interview could promote 'civil insurrection or disobedience'. (PINA) The military attempted to pressure three Radio Fiji journalists into disclosing the name of the military source who had passed them information concerning the composition of the interim government, it was reported on 25 October. Five days earlier, the editor of the state-owned station, **Francis Herman**, was telephoned by military chief Commodore Frank Bainimarama and asked to disclose the source of a report that elements of the military had opposed the appointment of Vice-President Ratu Jope Seniloli as acting president during a forthcoming visit to Australia. Herman refused and 90 minutes later he, along with news director **Vasiti Waqa** and reporter **Maca Lutunauga**, were taken into custody at gunpoint and interrogated for five hours. They were released but told that they might face charges under the security provisions of the emergency decree. The source was not revealed. (PINA) The editors of two journalists, charged with unlawful assembly with rebels, said that the reporters had been covering the takeover of an army camp in July and August, it was reported on 15 November. **Russell Hunter**, editor-in-chief of *Fiji Times*, and **Vasiti Waqa**, news director of Radio Fiji, said that reporters **Ruci Mafi** and **Theresa Ralogaivau** would be vigorously defended by their employers because they went to the camp for journalistic reasons. (PINA)

FRANCE

On 20 November a civil judge ordered US web company Yahoo Inc. to restrict French citizens from accessing sites that auction Nazi-related items in a case that set a precedent. The ruling, which dates back to May (*Index* 5/2000), was confirmed after a new testimony disproved Yahoo's claim that it was impossible to know the country of origin of those accessing US sites. Yahoo's French subsidiary already prohibits the posting of Nazi items, but this ruling forces a company established in the US to bar access to French citizens in accordance with their own national law. Yahoo now has three months in which to put a system in place, otherwise it will be fined FF100,000 (US$16,700) per day for non-compliance. The company is awaiting the written ruling before deciding whether to appeal. (*International Herald Tribune*)

GEORGIA

Antonio Russo, an Italian journalist with Radio Radicale, was found dead on 16 October on a roadside near the town of Gombori, about 50km north-east of Tbilisi. When local police and friends went to his apartment, the door was unlocked and his belongings were in disarray. His laptop, mobile phone, video camera and three videotapes were missing. Russo had been living in Tbilisi for two months while reporting on the conflict in Chechnya and was due to return to Italy on 18 October. An autopsy revealed that his death was caused either by a blow from a heavy instrument, or the impact of a vehicle. Two other journalists have died recently while reporting on human rights abuses in Chechnya – **Alexander Yefremov** and **Iskander Khatoni** (*Index* 6/2000). (*Observer*, RSF, WAN, CPJ)

GERMANY

The owner of a shop selling Nazi relics was forced to move her business to the Internet in mid-October after pressure from the police and locals in Berchtesgarden, near Hitler's former Alpine retreat. Locals were uncomfortable at the presence of **Pamela Korner**'s shop after they had expended so much energy trying to play down their region's association with Hitler. (*The Times*)

GHANA

Chris FM, a privately owned radio station in Berekum, was closed by armed soldiers on the orders of the Regional Security Council on 6 November. The closure followed allegations that an aspiring parliamentary candidate of the New Patriotic Party (NPP), **Nkrabeah Effah Darteh**, had used the station to incite his supporters to attack supporters of the ruling National Democratic Congress (NDC) a day earlier. Nineteen people were injured in the clash between supporters of the two parties. Darteh denied this allegation. The NPP is the largest opposition party in the country. (WAJA)

On 6 November the publisher and editor of the private *Ghanaian Chronicle*, **Nana Kofi Coomson**, and **Kwesi Koomson**, of the *Business Chronicle*, were arrested by armed officers of the Bureau of National Investigation (BNI) for having in their possession diskettes allegedly taken from the headquarters of the ruling NDC in Accra. The two were detained for about seven hours and denied food and water. George Pan Graham, the man alleged to have given the diskettes to the *Ghanaian Chronicle*, was remanded in custody by an Accra Circuit Tribunal. The authorities accuse the newspaper of purchasing stolen items. (WAJA)

On 8 November **Felix Odartey-Wellington**, a media critic for Ghana Television (GTV), was arrested by personnel of the BNI, chained and driven to police headquarters to be interrogated for describing the president as a 'conman' and 'fraudulent in politics'. Odartey-Wellington is the son of one of the officers killed when President Jerry Rawlings first came into power in 1979. He was granted bail of 50 million cedis (approximately US$7,223). (WAJA)

On 18 October the Supreme Court voted two to one against the public interest litigation that the **Narmada Bachao Andolan** (Save the Narmada Movement, or NBA) had filed against the Sardar Sarovar Dam Project in 1994. The decision was a major setback for the NBA because the court ignored the fact that the project does not have the acceptance of the estimated 500,000 people it would displace, and that the obligatory environmental impact appraisal has never been carried out. Moreover, not one of the people displaced so far has been adequately compensated, and there is no resettlement plan in place. (*Guardian*)

Father **Jacob Chittrinapilli** was abducted and killed in the state of Manipur on 3 December. He was taken from his church in Sugnu in the central district of Thoubal by two youths. No group has claimed responsibility. (BBC News Online)

INDONESIA

The Year of Living Dangerously, banned in 1982, was screened to a sell-out crowd at the Jakarta International Film Festival. The Censorship Board released the film on the condition that its single showing would be to a private audience only. (*Los Angeles Times*)

IRAN

Hassan Youssefi Eshkevari (*Index* 4/2000), a journalist with the suspended publications *Neshat* and *Iran-e-Farda*, was tried in camera before the Special Court for the Clergy from 7 to 15 October. Eshkevari is threatened with the death penalty for being a *mohareb* (fighter against god). (RSF)

On 18 October it was reported that six weekly publications, including *Milad* and *Jahan-i Pezeshki*, were banned by the Ministry of Islamic Culture and Guidance for 'ignoring repeated warnings'. (Journalists' Trade Union)

On 22 October *Sobh-e-Omid*, *Mihan* and *Sepideh-e Zendegi* were closed by the courts for 'violating the press law' and for using the logos of previously banned newspapers. Twenty-six other newspapers remain banned. (WAN, RSF)

Akbar Ganji (*Index* 4/2000), journalist for *Sobh-e-Emrouz*, began a hunger strike on 9 November – the day his trial began at the Revolutionary Court – in protest at the torture he has received since his arrest on 22 April. (RSF)

Khalil Rostamkhani, journalist for the *Daily News* and *Iran Echo*, appeared before the Revolutionary Court on 9 November. The prosecutor accused him of being a *mohareb* and asked for the death penalty. (RSF)

Satirical writer **Seyyed Ebrahim Nabavi** (*Index* 5/2000, 6/2000) pleaded guilty to insulting officials and propagating untruths, it was reported on 15 November. Nabavi was arrested on 12 August and accepted all but one of the charges against him, saying he 'had allowed himself to become angry and affected by public opinion and the extremism of some of his friends'. (BBC)

ISRAEL

A district court ruled on 24 October that the first ever performance of a work by Hitler's favourite composer, Richard Wagner, could go ahead. Judge Zaft acknowledged that Wagner was 'an extreme anti-semitic', but said 'the court should not interfere' in society's discussion of a wide variety of ideas. (*Guardian*)

It was reported on 16 November that Prime Minister Ehud Barak severely edited a document, entitled *The White Book,* written by Israeli intelligence detailing high-level corruption within the Palestinian Authority (PA). Barak was allegedly pressed by top Israeli negotiators to amend the book because, if the information was made public, 'it will be impossible to convince the Israeli public to reach an agreement with the PA'. This pro-Arafat censorship came the day after he backed down on his promise to declare a Palestinian state. (Middle East Realities)

KAZAKHSTAN

On 23 October, Almaty migration police officers went to the apartments of **Amirzhan Qosanov**, vice-chairman of the Kazakh Republican People's Party Executive Committee, and **Yermurat Bapi**, editor-in-chief of independent newspaper *SolDat*, and demanded their passports (*Index* 5/2000). According to Bapi, officials are trying to prevent him and Qosanov from travelling abroad to acquire additional information on some 'secret data' they had gained while working at official positions in the past. (RFE/RL)

KENYA

Photographer **Govedi Asuta** was recently barred from taking a picture of President Daniel arap Moi for the *Daily Nation* and ejected from a function at Kenyatta University. President Moi was making a visit to the university and conferring with doctoral degree graduates. Presidential guards also tried to snatch the camera from the journalist. Another photographer, working for Citizen Television, was also ejected. (NDIMA)

Four journalists on the *East African Standard* have been detained for motives which remain unclear, it was reported on 28 November. Photographer **Malachi Owino** was attacked in Kisumu, west of Nairobi, by 12 youths, allegedly members of the National Development Party, who broke his camera and left him with a head wound. On the same day, **Johann Wandetto**, **Jackson Orina** and **Osinde Obare**, journalists with the *People Daily*, the *Daily Nation*, *Kenya Times* and the *East African Standard* respectively, were arrested in Kitale. Though no clear motive has been made explicit, their incarceration seems connected with an article by Wandetto about Francis Lotodo, a controversial former minister who died on 8 November while preparing to undergo an operation. Wandetto had gone into hiding prior to his arrest. The minister's family had publicly threatened Wandetto on a previous occasion. (RSF)

KUWAIT

The daily *al-Siyassah* was suspended by the Council of Ministers for five days on 17 October, for insulting the Emir of Kuwait, Sheikh Jaber al-Ahmed al-Sabah. A 16 October article had quoted **Hamed al-Ali**, the secretary-general of the Islamist Salafiyya Movement, who alleged a 'secular conspiracy in the Gulf' and indirectly criticised the Emir for granting women the right to vote and participate in politics. Other private media covered the comments, but only *al-Siyassah* ran the story on its front page. It resumed publication on 23 October. (CPJ)

KYRGYSTAN

On 29 November editor-in-chief **Viktor Zapolsky** of independent newspaper *Delo N* announced that the Ministry of National Security had charged him and journalist **Vadim Notchevkin** with Clause 300 of the Criminal Code for 'divulging state secrets', by printing the full name of an MNS secret agent (*Index* 6/2000). (*Times of Central Asia*)

The young daily *Kapitalism's* life was cut short when it was shut down after issuing only its fourth edition. On 27 October government officials visited its editorial offices and demanded that all relevant documentation be produced, after which it was promptly closed. On 3 November, talks were held between publisher **Aibek Sydygaliev** and the assistant to the district prosecutor, Serguei Nikolaevich. Sydygaliev was told criminal proceedings would be brought against him on the grounds of slander. (CJES)

Aides of opposition candidate **Melis Eshimkanov** announced on 26 October that they have sued the independent TV station Pyramid because it refused to air commercials by Eshimkanov in spite of an agreement signed on 6 October. (CJES, RFE/RL).

On 25 October the Lenin District Court of Bishkek dismissed a lawsuit filed by presidential candidate **Omurbek Tekebaev** against the National TV and Radio Corporation. Since 9 October, the corporation has not aired commercials for Tekebaev. The court ruled that the case should be considered by the court of arbitration because of a contract signed by both parties on 12 October. On 24 October, Tekebaev won a similar case against Koort TV, and its president Temirbek Toktogaziev promised to resume Tekebaev's commercials from 26 October. (RFE/RL)

Independent newspaper *Litsa* was unable to distribute an edition scheduled for 23 October because printing firms refused to produce the issue. The editorial staff went to Kazakhstan, but print houses there had been instructed not to print newspapers from Kyrgystan. Eventually they printed the issue on photocopiers. (CJES)

On 20 October the Lenin District Court of Bishkek

ruled that opposition newspaper *Asaba* must pay 5 million soms (US$105,000) in compensation to Turdakun Usubaliev (*Index* 5/2000). This came a week after the paper had filed a counter-claim against Usubaliev that accused him of insulting the paper and its journalist in his claim. Usubaliev was ordered to pay the paper 50,000 soms (US$1,000). Usbaliev, an MP and former First Secretary of the Central Committee of the Kyrgystan Communist Party, sued the paper for insulting him regularly for the last eight years. Several journalists on the paper who criticised him must pay him between 1,000 and 1,500 soms each. Editor **Ernis Asek Uulu** said he would appeal. (CJES, RFE/RL)

On 17 October the Pervomai District Court fined independent newspaper *Res Publica* 20,000 soms (US$400). Editor-in-chief **Zamira Sodykova** and reporter **Yrysbek Omurzakoy** were also fined 2,000 soms (US$40) and 3,000 soms (US$60) respectively. Omurzakoy wrote an article accusing a former employee of the Kyrgyz Committee for Human Rights (KCHR), Sardarbek Botaliev, of organising a duplicate committee under the same name, which was more loyal to the government. After numerous protests from abroad the Ministry of Justice was forced to re-register the original KCHR. (CJES, RFE/RL)

LAOS

A warning was issued in the *Vientiane Times* on 26 October instructing people 'not to use the Internet in the wrong

way'. The guidelines of 'proper' use were created by the National Internet Management Committee, which has banned 'misleading news stories to create … doubts among the public, at home or abroad'. (CPJ)

MACEDONIA

Gunshots were fired into the front door of journalist **Aleksandar Comovski** in the early hours of 27 November. On the same day TV A1 and TV Sitel's transmitters were left without electricity, resulting in their inability to broadcast outside Skopje. TV Sitel also received a bomb threat that day. (GHM)

MALAWI

Vice-President Aleke Banda of Malawi's ruling United Democratic Front (UDF) is to sue the Lilongwe-based independent weekly *Chronicle* over a story claiming he misappropriated public funds. The newspaper's managing editor said he stood by the story, but that it had not directly implicated Banda in corruption. (MISA)

MALAYSIA

On 22 November **Penerbitan Pemuda** was charged with printing and publishing tabloid magazine *Haraki* without a permit. The publishing house responsible is owned by **Ahmad Lutfi Othman** (*Index* 6/2000). Pemuda could be sentenced to three years in jail, a fine of RM20,000, or both, under the 1984 Printing Presses and Publications Act. (www.malaysiakini.com)

MALI

On 30 August a journalist with the private biweekly *L'Indépendent*, **Chahana Takiou**, was assaulted by a member of parliament for the ruling Democratic Alliance of Mali. In the attack by MP Mamadou Gassama, Takiou was almost strangled and nearly lost consciousness. The journalist, who was covering a story within the National Assembly chamber, had previously written an article in *L'Indépendent* which uncovered a case of political corruption. (RSF)

MAURITANIA

On 6 November the editor of the weekly *L'Opinion Libre*, **Ely Ould Nafa**, was assaulted with clubs outside his home by two unidentified men who left him with a fractured arm and severe bruising. One of the attackers was arrested that evening. An investigation has been launched, but as yet no motive for the assault is known. Since January 2000 seven newspapers, including *L'Eveil Hebdo* (*Index* 3/2000), have been banned or seized. (RSF)

MOROCCO

Agence France-Presse's Rabat correspondent **Claude Juvenal** was expelled from the country on 6 November on the orders of the Minister of Communications, Mohamed Achaari. Juvenal's press accreditation had been withdrawn two days earlier after he was accused of 'straying from the professional code of ethics'. He was subsequently told by the authorities that he had no business staying in Morocco, and was ordered to leave the country. Although the authorities gave no reasons for Juvenal's deportation, it is thought that he had infuriated the government by exposing corruption in the military services. (RSF, WAN)

On 2 December Communications Minister Mohamed Achaari announced a permanent ban on three weekly newspapers. *Le Journal*, *Assahifa* and *Demain* were accused of 'deliberately attacking the most sacred institutional foundations of the country' after publishing a letter written by exiled opposition leader **Mohamed Basri**, in which he directly implicated Prime Minister Abderrahmane Youssoufi in an attempted coup against King Hassan II in 1972. **Ali Lmrabet**, the editor of *Demain*, claimed that this was the latest of a series of acts taken by the authorities to impede the publication of his newspaper. (MISA, RSF)

NAMIBIA

On 3 November senior Namibian Broadcasting Corporation (NBC) employee **Norah Appolus** reached a settlement with the NBC after challenging her removal as head of the news and current affairs division (*Index* 6/2000). Appolus claims she was demoted to a more junior position for political reasons. (MISA)

On 4 November the leader of the ruling South West African People's Organisation (SWAPO) Youth League, Paulus Kapia, accused the *Namibian* newspaper of destroying 'the good image of our SWAPO government' and said that 'we must put a stop [to people] reading it'. Two days later officials from the government and SWAPO distanced themselves from Kapia's statements, saying they did not represent official policy. (MISA)

NIGER

Three journalists were arrested between 23 and 25 October and held in Niamey civil prison. **Sumana Maiga**, **Dahirou Gouro** and **Salif Dago**, the founder, managing editor and reporter, respectively, of the private weekly *L'Enquêteur*, were accused of 'lying' and disturbing the peace. Their arrest related to an article about a ten-year border dispute with Bénin over the island of Lété. At their hearing on 16 November, Gouro and Dago were each given a six-month suspended sentence and fined, while Maiga was sentenced to eight months in prison. Severe irregularities were noted at the trial, including the fact that the court had been unable to establish that the journalists acted in bad faith. Since 25 October *L'Enquêteur* has failed to appear. (RSF, CPJ)

NIGERIA

Under new laws which will take effect from 26 November, journalists in the state of Kano who are found guilty of publishing 'offensive' stories are to be caned publicly under the Islamic legal code of Sharia. The punishments, which can take the form of 60

Quality in life

The *Index* Courage in Journalism award, sponsored by *The Economist*, is dedicated to unsung journalists or editors overseas, working in an isolation that is vast by comparison with our own, but who somehow fulfil the highest aspirations of the profession.

Last year's winner was Zeljko Kopanja, co-founder and editor of the largest circulation daily in the Republika Serbska part of Bosnia. He lost both legs in a car-bomb attack following his investigation into Serb killings of Bosnian Muslims during the 1992–95 war. Previous winners have hailed from Sierra Leone and Samoa.

This year's winner was shot and killed by unknown gunmen on 22 November. I never met the man, but I was immediately transported back to the moment in 1993 when I first heard of the assassination of ANC activist Chris Hani. In those faltering months after the end of apartheid, Hani stood tall as a bridge between the old guard and the boys in the townships with nothing left to lose. His killing was a dreadful squandering of more than hope, more than youth. It was the murder of a certain quality in life.

I feel the same about Carlos Cardoso, a journalist in Mozambique who founded the world's first faxed daily newspaper in 1992, and then set up the business daily *Metical*, whose offices are close by where his murderers lay in wait. In the absence of any robust opposition, journalists like Carlos naturally emerged as chief critics of government policy. At the time of his death, he was investigating the 1997 privatisation of the Commercial Bank of Mozambique and the alleged theft of US$10m by those involved in the process. He stuck to his story, despite being invited by the Attorney General's office to reveal his sources in May (*Index* 4/2000). He never did.

His picture in the next day's obituary showed a man with dancing eyes, in the middle of his road through life, a face that also made his two kids' eyes light up, that was tender, fun-loving and industrious. So someone decided to kill it, because it contained the same honest evidence of that certain quality in a life.

The 2000 'Courage in Journalism' prize is – with deepest regret – awarded to Nina Berg, widow of Carlos Cardoso. ❏

MG

strokes of the cane, are to be televised, reported and witnessed by the editor of the offending journalist. The new measures are said to be necessary 'to ensure that journalists publish only the truth as the Sharia law had no distinction between the highly placed and the masses'. (Nigerian Media Monitor)

PAKISTAN

The magistrate of Skardu district banned the weekly newspaper *K2* on 17 October for publishing 'objectionable material, promoting anti-Pakistan feelings and advocating [the] curtailment of territories'. He rebuked **Raja Hussain Khan Maqpoon**, editor of *K2*, for publishing an article last April, entitled 'A Sovereign Gilgit, Baltistan: A Review', in which a former student leader advocated the independence of the region. The magistrate also chastised him for publishing an article in August about a pro-independence demonstration by Baltistani people. (RSF, Pakistan Press Foundation)

A possible suicide bomb attack occurred in Karachi on 6 November in the advertising offices of the press group that publishes the dailies *Nation* in English and *Nawa-i-Waqt* in Urdu. An unnamed woman, who is believed to have carried in the bomb, entered the advertising manager's office a few minutes before the blast. Three people were killed in the attack, including the unknown woman and **Najmul Hasan Zaidi**, the staff manager. A fourth person, **Sajid Mehmood**, died from his injuries on 11 November.

Although no one has claimed responsibility for the attack, the *Nation* recently published articles about corruption in the army, and its editor, **Arif Nizami**, has accused the Mutthahida Quami Movement of responsibility. (RSF, BBC News Online, Pakistan Press Foundation, CPJ, *International Herald Tribune*)

Recent Publication: *Reform or Repression? Post-Coup Abuses in Pakistan (Human Rights Watch, October 2000, pp20)*

PALESTINE

Atta Oweisat, a photographer for Israeli press agency Zoom 77, was beaten on 4 October by undercover Israeli security agents while covering the funeral of a Palestinian in Jabel Moukaber, Jerusalem. He believes the attack may have been motivated by his filming a week earlier of Israeli agents in Jerusalem's Shufat refugee camp. He said: 'My presence as a photojournalist has been a nuisance for [Israeli undercover agents] who infiltrate among the local Palestinians during demonstrations and who are strongly opposed to their identities being exposed.' (CPJ)

On 7 October **Khalid Suleiman Amaryeh**, publisher and editor of the bi-weekly *Hebron Times*, was detained by Palestinian police following his live appearance on the Gulf-based satellite news station Al-Shareqah. Amaryeh had been criticising the Palestine Authority (PA) for its corruption and negotiations with Israel, and had called for the release of impris-

oned Hamas activists. He was released after 30 hours in custody and his forced signing of a pledge to abide by Palestinian information laws. (CPJ)

The camera lens of **Luc Delahaye**, a freelance photographer with Magnum photo agency and *Newsweek* magazine, was hit by an Israeli rubber-coated metal bullet on 9 October. He was filming clashes in Ramallah and his camera was destroyed. The next day his head was grazed by another bullet, and a week later he was hit on the forehead by a third rubber bullet while photographing a protestor who had just been hit in the head by a live round. (CPJ)

On 12 October a Palestinian mob prevented several journalists from filming the killing of two Israeli soldiers in Ramallah. An ABC cameraman was kicked in the groin and stomach, British freelance photographer **Mark Seager** was assaulted and had his camera smashed, AFP cameraman **Patrick Baz** had a camera snatched from him, and other journalists were prevented from filming the incident. (CPJ)

On 12 October Israeli helicopters opened fire on two transmission towers and other technical facilities used by the Voice of Palestine in Ramallah. The army justified the attack by charging that the station had incited Palestinians to commit violence by broadcasting pictures of Palestinians dragging an effigy of an Israeli soldier. (CPJ)

On 17 October Reuters photographer **Mahfouz Abu Turk** was wounded in the hand by a rubber-coated metal bullet fired by Israeli troops.

Testimony

Eyewitnesses

'I was filming the crowd during Friday prayers when the clashes took place by the Magharbeh Gate. All of a sudden the soldiers approached me and began beating me with bats and sticks on my head and shoulders. I ran towards the Gate and from there I was [taken], bleeding from my head and right leg, to Hadassah Hospital.' Khaled Zeghari, Reuters cameraman.

'When I began to take pictures, seven [Israeli security agents] attacked me, threw me to the ground and started beating me and stepping on me, trying hard to pull the camera away from me. Then a Border Patrol soldier came and held me by the neck and one of the [agents] stood on my stomach.' Atta Oweisat, Zoom 77 photographer.

'In the three incidents I was definitely targeted by the soldiers, but I cannot say if I was targeted as a human being, or as a journalist.' Luc Delahaye, Magnum photographer.

'It was obvious [we were journalists]. We were wearing white helmets and flak jackets. I got [a rubber-coated metal bullet] on my finger . . . I would not complain if I was in the middle of the demonstration, [but we were] in an empty field.' Patrick Baz, AFP photographer.

'From where he was standing, only those in front of him could have hit him. And those in front of him were Israeli soldiers,' said *Paris-Match* deputy editor Patrick Jarnoux of reporter Jacques-Marie Bourget. 'A 57-year-old man can't easily be mistaken for a 15-year-old rock thrower.'

'While I was in a semi-standing position, holding the camera and with my back facing Israeli tanks . . . I felt a sudden strike to the right side of my back. I thought that it must be a rubber bullet but, when I felt the blood coming from the site of injury, I realised that it was live.' Benjamin Wedemann, CNN correspondent.

'The settlers attack us for two reasons: because we're journalists and because we're Palestinians. The most important thing for the settlers is to stop the cameras from showing their activities to the world and the Israeli public.' Mazen Dana, Reuters cameraman.

'We don't understand why we were targeted since we are far from the lines of confrontation and there was absolutely no fire coming from the vicinity of the university compound,' Daoud Kuttab, director of the Institute of Modern Media. ❏

Compiled by **Neil Sammonds**

He had been covering clashes which had broken out after the funeral of a Palestinian boy. (CPJ)

AFP photographer **Patrick Baz** was shot in the finger with a rubber-coated metal bullet fired by an Israeli soldier while covering clashes in Ramallah on 18 October. Baz was standing with another photographer at the time. (CPJ)

On 18 October the Israeli Press Office revoked the accreditation of **Riccardo Cristiano**, a journalist with Italian state-TV network RAI. It followed the publication of a letter by Cristiano in which he stated that the filming of the lynching of two Israeli soldiers in Ramallah had not been done by RAI. (CPJ)

On 23 October AP reporter and photographer **Nasser Shiyoukhi** was prevented from entering the village of Sumoua by Israeli soldiers who also confiscated his Israeli press card. (CPJ)

Bruno Stephens, a freelance photographer working with *Libération* and *Stern*, was grazed in the throat by a bullet while covering clashes in Ramallah on 23 October. Stephens was standing away from Palestinians in a group of journalists. He believes the bullet was fired by Israeli troops. (CPJ)

Jacques-Marie Bourget, a reporter for *Paris-Match*, was hit in the chest by a bullet and seriously injured while covering clashes on 23 October. Bourget was standing among journalists and other bystanders. Colleagues believe the shot, which entered his lung, was fired by Israeli soldiers. (CPJ)

Suleiman al-Shafei, a reporter and cameraman for Israeli Channel 2, was detained by Israeli police on 31 October and interrogated over his journey to Gaza. He refused to answer questions and was finally released on bail, but his footage of the Israeli bombing of the PNA offices in Gaza was confiscated. A virtually identical incident occurred on 2 November. (CPJ)

On 31 October CNN's Cairo bureau chief **Ben Wedeman** was hit in the back by a round at the Karni crossing between Gaza and Israel. During a lull in a clash he had his back to Israeli troops and the shot passed through his flak jacket. (CPJ)

Freelance photographer **Yola Monakhov** was shot in the lower abdomen by a round fired by an Israeli soldier in Bethlehem, while she covered a clash for AP on 11 November. Monakhov sustained serious injuries to her bladder and other organs, and her pelvis was fractured in several places. (CPJ)

On 12 November Reuters cameraman **Mazen Dana** (*Index* 6/2000) was blocked by soldiers from entering the old city of Hebron, while accompanying the visit of UN Commissioner for Human Rights Mary Robinson. After protests by Robinson, Dana was allowed to proceed but his car was then attacked by Jewish settlers, and then he was detained at the local police station for one and a half hours. (CPJ)

On 12 November the car of Reuters cameramen **Abdel Rahim Quisini** and **Nasser Ishtayyeh** was attacked by Jewish settlers as they travelled towards Nablus. Quisini and Ishtayyeh say they were attacked by about 40 settlers while Israeli soldiers looked on, even though the car carried Israeli licence plates and a 'press' sticker. (CPJ)

PA security forces raided the private, Bethlehem-based TV station Al-Roa' on 15 November and temporarily forced it off the air. Soldiers beat director **Hamdi Farraj** and other members of staff, and allegedly threatened to shoot them and destroy the station's equipment. Transmission was soon resumed but two days later police arrived again with a letter from PA police chief Ghazi Jebali and another from Arafat saying 'do what you think is necessary'. Staff reported that the authorities accused the station of 'promoting religious strife'. (CPJ)

On 22 November a tank shell was fired from the Psagot settlement at the Al Quds University building which holds the Al-Quds Educational Television station. The station was broadcasting live the Israeli shelling of Ramallah. The shelling caused a small fire but no one was injured. (AMARC)

PAPUA NEW GUINEA

It was reported on 20 November that journalists from an independent television station, EMTV, were attacked and forced to flee by trade unionists taking part in a march against government policies in Port Moresby, the capital, four days earlier. The marchers had claimed that the media was biased against them. Cameraman **Sai Nou** needed four stitches to a head wound and reporter **Jacqueline Tarue** suffered minor injuries and lost her glasses. (PINA)

PERU

On 10 October **Segundo Jara Montejo**, a correspondent for the National Radio Co-ordinating Committee and the Huánaco regional daily, was attacked by police officers while covering a demonstration by coca farmers protesting against the eradication of their crops. Jara Montejo was hit by one of the tear-gas bombs, which were also being thrown at the farmers, suffering injury to his right leg. The president of the Alto Huallaga Human Rights Commission, Rosalie Storck Salazar, confirmed that Montejo had been intentionally hit while filming. (IPYS)

Journalist **José del Parraguez Peréz** was attacked by eight unknown assailants on 25 October. Host of *Análisis*, broadcast on Radio FVC in Nueva Cajamarca, he had been previously warned to stop his investigations into state corruption. Although he filed a complaint about the attack, no police officer has yet responded. (IFJ)

Unidentified individuals broke into the offices of Panamericana Televisión in Tacna on 16 October and stole around US$10,000 worth of editing equipment, 24 hours after the TV station had broadcast a report on alleged police excesses during a local protest march in September. Panamericana's Tacna-based correspondent, **Emilio Vargas Barreda**, reported on the brutal beating suffered by **Pastor Pilco Cotrado** at the hands of police. (IPYS)

On 22 October unidentified individuals broke the windows and destroyed the transmission equipment of Laser radio station in the city of Sihuas. Journalist **Javier Alejos**, who hosts the station's news programme, *El Chasqui*, claims that the attack was ordered by local mayor Hermenegildo Morillo. According to Alejos, the mayor had days before issued a death threat against him for reporting on irregularities at the local municipality. (IFJ)

The government issued a ministerial resolution on 7 November restoring Peruvian citizenship to exiled media businessman **Baruch Ivcher Bronstein**. The move followed an agreement struck between government and opposition parties at a round-table discussion overseen by the Organisation of American States (OAS). However, the government has still to issue a supreme resolution backing the recommendations put forward by the Inter-American Commission on Human Rights to hand control of Canal 2 television station back to Ivcher (*Index* 4/1997, 6/1997, 1/1998, 2/1998, 3/1998, 4/1998, 5/1998, 6/1998, 2/1999, 4/1999, 5/1999, 1/2000). (IFJ)

On 13 November Héctor Huansi, governor of the Barranca district, verbally assaulted journalists **Eduardo Geovanni Acate Coronel** and **Marco Antonio Bisalote Ubillus**. Coronel is the host of *El Estelo*, a programme broadcast on Radio Oriente in the Loreto department. Huanasi appeared on the news programme and began to insult the Peruvian press, in partic-

ular those critical of the regime. He described the independent daily *El Commercio* and opposition dailies *La República* and *Liberación* as 'tabloids used to deceive the people'. When two journalists asked him to leave, he threatened to file complaints and to attack them physically. Huansi requested the director of Canal 19, the regional government television station, to fire his employer Ubillus on the grounds that his editorial line did not comply with the government. (IPYS)

A group of police officers attacked photojournalist **Willy Zarate Ajaujo** on 15 November. Documenting the oppression suffered by construction workers for the daily *El Tío*, police threatened, insulted and ordered him to leave upon discovering that he was a reporter. When he refused, the police attacked him with a tear-gas bomb, which threw him to the ground. *El Tío* has demanded an immediate investigation into the incident. (IPS)

Two unknown individuals attacked a reporter from Radio Lider en Arequipa, **Roxana Aquino Garcia**, as she was leaving the National San Agustín University Stadium on 16 November. Her attackers are thought to be linked to Manuel Saiki Rios, the treasurer of the Melgar football club. Aquino had been reporting irregularities in the transfer of club player Ysrael Zuniga to Britain's Coventry City. Saiki, as treasurer of the club, is held to have the main responsibility for the flawed transactions. Following her attack, Aquino reported the incident to the sub-prefect of

Arequipa and asked for protection. (IFJ)

Since August, **Marilú Gambini Lostanau**, a Chimbote-based correspondent for the daily *Liberación*, has come under sustained harassment from suspected members of the Peruvian National Police (PNP) and the National Intelligence Service (SIN). The journalist, who has been investigating cases of alleged corruption involving PNP and SIN officers, has received threatening phone calls and had her home ransacked. On 18 November her two-and-a-half-year-old son was kidnapped for ten hours. The child reappeared unharmed with a written warning saying that, next time, the consequences would be more serious. (IPYS)

PHILIPPINES

Journalist and broadcaster **Olipio 'Jun' Jalapit** was murdered on 17 November in Pagadian City. Working for the private radio station DXPR, he had received death threats because of his broadcasts condemning corruption in Zamboanga province. (RSF)

ROMANIA

Anghel Stanciu, vice-president of Romania's far-right Mare Party, made threats to journalists in a 29 November statement in Iasi, declaring: 'We must intern journalists in work camps.' After Agence France-Presse reporter **Stefan Susai** quoted this and other comments, he was ordered to retract by local Mare leaders. After refusing, Susai received a number of anonymous tele-

phone threats. Stanciu later denied making such comments, despite the fact that they had been recorded. (RSF)

RUSSIA

An order was issued to arrest Media-MOST's head **Vladimir Gusinsky** for fraud because he failed to comply with a summons to appear before a court on 13 November (*Index* 4/2000, 5/2000). Gusinsky sent a message via his lawyers saying he had no intention of appearing because he believes he is being persecuted for political reasons. Deputy Prosecutor General Vasili Kolmogorov made it clear that, if Gusinsky sought refuge in Israel where he is also a citizen, Russia would insist on his extradition. (RFE/RL)

The management of Sberbank (Saving Bank) subsequently demanded that the Media-MOST group return loans of US$100 million even though the term of the credit has not been reached. The Sberbank's management doubts the group's creditworthiness as the demands of gas giant Gazprom, which took over the Gusinsky media empire in July, will significantly affect Media-MOST's profitability. Shares of the Echo of Moscow radio station, which is part of the Media-MOST group, were seized in accordance with the decision of the Arbitrage Court on the Gazprom's claim. NTV's satellites could face seizure if Vneshekonombank (Bank for Foreign Trade) demands payment of US$30 million by the Arbitrage Court. (EIM)

Magomet Tekeyev, editor-in-chief of the independent daily *Gorskiye Vedomosti* in the republic of Karatchayev-Tcherkessie, was brutally and repeatedly assaulted with a club and a bag filled with nails and screws in front of his residence in the capital, Tcherkesk, on 14 October. In his articles Tekeyev repeatedly denounced corruption in the top echelons of the republic. (RSF, WAN)

Accused of conspiring to murder journalist **Dimitry Kholodov** in 1994, five former military intelligence officers and the head of a bodyguard agency went on trial in Moscow on 9 November. The suspects allegedly killed Kholodov with a suitcase bomb to impress their superiors, whom the journalist was investigating for corruption among the military leadership. The trial, which was closed to the press and public, was adjourned shortly after proceedings. (BBC, RFE/RL)

A criminal case was launched against independent weekly *Versija* (Version) on 10 November, following the publication of satellite photographs which showed a damaged US submarine at a Norwegian naval base which had supposedly collided with the nuclear submarine Kursk (*Index* 6/2000). Staff were questioned by Federal Security Service (FSS) between 10 and 17 November, starting with a four-hour interrogation of editor **Dmitry Filimonov**. On the same day his desktop computer was confiscated. The FFS are interested in the origin of the photograph but, according to Filimonov, he received the images from an unknown person. A number of documents were seized from the office and, on 17 November, FSS officers revisited *Versija* and removed more documents along with a computer from the design department. (GDF)

Legislation banning the public use of the swastika and other Nazi symbols was pushed through at the request of Prime Minister Mikhail Kasyanov. It was reported on 8 November that several extremist groups, including Russian National Unity, use the symbols even though they were banned in the mid-1990s. (RFE/RL)

Journalist **Grigori Pasko** was sent back before Vladivostok Military Court by the Supreme Court's military section, it was reported on 21 November, after already spending two years in jail on the basis of unfounded accusations. Pasko was accused of gathering state secrets with the intention of transmitting them to foreign organisations. At the time of his arrest in 1997, Pasko had been a correspondent with *Boevaya Vakhta* aboard the Russian tanker TNT 27 and had filmed liquid radioactive waste being disposed of in the Sea of Japan. (RSF)

Adam Tepsurgayev, a freelance cameraman working in Chechnya, was assassinated on 21 November inside a house in the town of Alkhan-Kala south of Grozny. According to Tepsurgayev's brother, who was injured in the attack, armed men speaking Chechen burst into the house and started shooting. Tepsurgayev worked for a number of media outlets including Reuters. A Kremlin spokesman said the journalist did not have accreditation from the authorities. (RSF)

SAMOA

Opposition leader Tuiatua Tupua Tamasese Efi has accused the government of intimidating the media by making public funds available for the prime minister and members of the cabinet to sue for defamation, it was reported on 27 November. The measure was introduced two years ago by then prime minister Tofilau Eti Alesana, when he was suing the *Samoa Observer* newspaper for defamation. Tuiatua added that at least 1.3m tala (US\$379,111) of taxpayers' money was used for Tofilau's legal fees. (Pacific Media Watch)

SERBIA

It has emerged that the management of Radio Television Serbia (RTS) were made aware of the imminent NATO air strike 24 hours before it took place on 23 April. The RTS Strike Committee uncovered information revealing that former director Dragoljub Milanovic was told of the precise date and time of the attack and failed to evacuate staff from the building. Slobodan Sisic, the lawyer representing the families of the RTS employees who were killed, found an official memo written by four senior RTS guards on 2 April. The memo revealed that Milanovic had refused to issue an order that called for employees and equipment to be moved to the Kosutnjak centre. The investigation is now based on 16 counts of premeditated murder against eight former members of staff. (ANEM)

UN police officers arrested the suspects involved in the murder of Sefki Popova (*Index* 6/2000) on 14 October as part of a programme of raids in Pristina. (ANEM)

Mira Maslarevic and **Nada Hadzimurtezic**, editor-in-chief and deputy editor of Radio Cacak, resigned on 17 October in protest at the removal of Television S equipment and and its transfer to Television Cacak, controlled by the local government. (ANEM)

Journalist **Zoran Lukovic** (*Index* 3/2000, 5/2000) was pardoned and released from prison on 21 October, only a week after the Justice Ministry refused his request for parole. Lukovic, a journalist with the daily *Dnevni Telegraf*, spent two months in prison after his conviction last year on libel charges for allegedly slandering former deputy premier Milovan Bojic. (AIM, ANEM)

Jagodina Municipal Court issued an order on 22 October for the confiscation of the passport of journalist **Milovan Brkic**. Brkic was charged several months ago with causing damage to the reputation of Slobodan Milosevic, and this order was issued to prevent him from leaving the country until criminal proceedings had been completed. The order was apparently issued on 29 May. (ANEM)

RTS dropped the series *Images and Words of Hate* from its programming in the last week of October, reportedly as a result of pressure from the Democratic Opposition of Serbia. It is seen as an attempt to cover up the network's involvement in the instigation of war crimes, particularly as the belligerent comments of former director Milorad Vucelic were discussed in programmes to be aired. (ANEM)

Employees of private Radio Caricingrad have decided to revoke their membership of the Serbian Socialist Party and the Yugoslav Left. Editor-in-chief **Srdjan Zivkovic** stated on 28 October that their motive in joining the parties in the first place had been 'to obtain frequencies more easily'. (ANEM)

Belgrade-based Humanitarian Law Centre has received a document relating to the murder in April 1999 of *Dnevni Telegraf* owner and editor-in-chief **Slavko Curuvija** (*Index* 3/1999, 6/1999). The document from the Belgrade State Security Service relates to the undercover surveillance that was organised at the command of Rade Markovic, chief of the State Security Service. The document says that undercover agents were withdrawn from their duties by their head of department only a few minutes before the editor was shot dead. The Humanitarian Law Centre announced on 31 October that it intended to file a complaint against the State Security Chiefs, charging them with Curuvija's murder. (*Observer*)

On 1 November Belgrade police detained *Ndeljni Telegraf* assistant editor **Milos Antic**, without giving reasons. It is presumed that his arrest is connected with articles he wrote about orders issued by Milosevic to the Army Chief of Staff to 'liquidate' 50 people, one of whom was President Vojislav Kostunica. (ANEM)

Poet, paediatrician and human rights activist **Flora Brovina** (*Index* 6/2000) was released from Posarevac prison at 3.30pm on 1 November. The order for her release was issued by President Kostunica himself. She had spent 18 months in prison. Her release has raised hopes for the release of the 850 Kosovar Albanians who are being held in Serbian prisons. (ANEM, Amnesty, Writers in Prison Committee)

RTS employees learned that colleagues who were members of the Socialist Party of Serbia and the Yugoslav Left received significantly larger salaries. RTS director Dragoljub Milanovic, editors Milorad Komrakov and Tatjana Lenard, as well as many other journalists and technicians received proportionally higher remuneration than their colleagues. The RTS Strike Committee demanded that all managers, department heads and compromised journalists be dismissed from their positions. (ANEM, *International Herald Tribune*)

Dragoljub Todorovic, lawyer for former *Politika* director Hadzi-Dragan Antic, announced on 3 November that he had filed criminal charges against 'all authors and editors of information containing untruths, lies and libel' about his client. He also announced plans to reveal information that would present the last decade's workings of the pro-Milosevic *Politka* and its staff 'in a new light'. Antic filed criminal charges against several senior executives and journalists from the company, it was announced on 14 November. He alleges that his reputation was damaged in articles published in *Politika* and *Danas* that claimed he abused his authority within the company. Those charged include *Politika's* new director, **Darko Ribnikar**. Antic's lawyer announced his intention to file more charges against journalists from dailies *Borba* and *Vecernje novosti*. (ANEM)

On 4 November Federal Minister of Telecommunications Boris Tadic, announced his plan to call a public frequency tender, which in his belief would create a stable media. All municipalities would retain their own media, and others would be offered on the free market. When reminded of those radio stations which had been denied frequencies in the past, he promised to look into the matter. The next day he emphasised his commitment to returning confiscated frequencies to their rightful owners, and urged that all frequencies should be considered national property that is leased, rather than sold. (ANEM)

President of Montenegrin People's Party Dragan Soc called for the dismissal of Montenegrin Television's editorial staff. According to Soc, the station spreads anti-Serb sentiment and promotes the ideas of Montenegrin independence. Quoted in Belgrade daily *Glas javnosti* on 5 November, Soc warned that his party would not resume talks with the ruling coalition on a Montenegrin referendum

MIROSLAV FILIPOVIC
Tito's children

Every young journalist at the start of his career imagines himself a kind of Hamlet who wants to change things. I tried to help to make things better. I worked for the *Ibarske novosti* in Kraljevo, doing interviews and commentaries on questions of state, but I resigned in 1993 and didn't do any journalism for the next five years. In that period I wrote a book about the history of Kraljevo and its airline factory, which my wife and I financed ourselves.

There used to be a strong belief in Serbia that there are circumstances in which a journalist is obliged to lie, usually in the name of patriotism. Whenever I wrote, I always asked myself what gave a journalist the right to lie to himself, or to his readers. I believe that there is nothing that would compel me to lie, or which makes lying acceptable.

In 1999, after the huge gap in my journalism, it was time to start writing again. My home town of Kraljevo was full of stories since, on average, one man from every family had been recruited into the forces that went to Kosovo. I sensed a really good story there and started following the path of the most interesting ones. I found three media houses that would accept my style of writing and I sought out Agence France-Presse and Institute of War and Peace Reporting.

As far as the local newspapers are concerned, they are still not ready to publish the stories that I write. Even two months after the changes in Serbia, none of my texts has been published in the national media. The majority of adults were educated when Marshal Tito was still in power and they don't know how to act differently. The priority is to educate young journalists in western principles of journalism, hopefully several hundred of them. The people that can make real change are governments. I am travelling around Europe now, in a way to use you and your colleagues to alert them and show them more effective ways in which they can help Serbia and its people. ❑

This is an extract from an interview with **Miroslav Filipovic,** *who was released from Nis Military Prison in October following the overthrow of Slobodan Milosevic* (Index 4/2000, 5/2000, 6/2000). *Edited by Louise Finer* unless the sackings took place. (ANEM)

The appearance of Human Rights Foundation director **Natasa Kandic** *(Index 6/2000)* on Television Novi Sad on 10 November provoked a bomb threat and numerous insulting messages from viewers. (ANEM)

A misdemeanour case brought against the weekly *Vranjske novine* under the Public Information Act was dropped on 10 November. The case had been filed by Vranje Lumber Camp in response to a 2 November article about the financial dealings of its senior officials. Meanwhile, the Yugoslav Legal Experts Committee for Human Rights are demanding that the Constitutional Court examine the legality of the Public Information Act, which they believe to be unconstitutional. On 10 November the committee proposed that the 1991 Information Act be reinstated until an alternative is written. (ANEM)

The joint initiative by President Kostunica and the Serbian Orthodox Church to introduce religious instruction in schools was criticised on 21 November by the Serbian Helsinki Human Rights Board. The initiative, they said, would 'seriously violate the principles of a secular state' and would take a step towards the indoctrination of children. (BETA)

SPAIN

An attempt to assassinate **Aurora Intxausti**, journalist with Madrid daily *El País*, and **Juan Palomo**, journalist with private television station

Antena 3 on 10 November failed. Two kilograms of explosives were hidden at the couple's front door, but they did not fully detonate when the couple opened it. The Basque government's Minister of the Interior, Jaime Mayor Oreja, said that the attack was undoubtedly the work of the Basque separatist group, ETA. Intxausti is one of 40 journalists who have been denounced in the Basque political magazine *Ardibeltza*. (RSF)

Journalist, professor at Barcelona University and ex-health minister **Ernest Lluch** was shot dead in a Barcelona car park on 21 November. The attack bore the hallmark of ETA, which has claimed responsibility for the murder of 20 politicians, police and journalists this year. (*Guardian*)

Thousands of people demonstrated in Donostia on 25 November against government attempts to close the magazine *Ardibeltza* and curtail their freedom of expression. (*Gara*)

SRI LANKA

Following the parliamentary elections on 10 October, two international election observer delegations were severely criticised by local monitors for endorsing the results. Despite widespread reports of vote-rigging and election-related violence in which more than 70 people were killed, the EU and the UK-Sri Lanka Parliamentary Group both concluded that the vote was a 'reasonable' reflection of the will of the people. The Colombo-based Centre for Monitoring Election Violence (CMEV), on the other hand,

said that the nature and extent of violations in 17 of the 160 electoral divisions were so widespread and serious that the final outcome in those areas was 'utterly meaningless'. (*Sri Lanka Monitor*, Centre For Monitoring Election Violence, National Peace Council, *Island, Sunday Leader*)

On 26 October 27 former Tamil Tiger rebels were killed and 13 wounded by a Sinhalese mob that stormed their rehabilitation camp in Bindunuwewa. Anti-Tamil sentiment in the area was reportedly whipped up by a poster campaign, which incited locals to attack the ex-rebels in the camp. (*Frontline*, *Sri Lanka Monitor*)

An unidentified Sinhalese-speaking man was arrested on 19 November for verbally abusing President Chandrika Kumaratunga during a phone-in talk show on state-controlled radio. Police said that the man would likely be charged with criminal defamation under laws which make it an offence to bring the head of state into public ridicule. (Reuters, Agence France-Presse)

Sinha Ranatunge, editor of the *Sunday Times*, had his one-year suspended prison sentence for defamation against President Chandrika Kumaratunga upheld by the appeals court on 5 December. Ranatunge was convicted in July 1997 for a gossip column about the president that appeared in February 1995 (*Index* 2/1995, 3/1995, 5/1997, 2/1998). (Agence France-Presse)

Recent Publications: *Final Report of the European Union's Observation Mission to Sri*

PRASANNA VITHANAGE
Vacuum in Jaffna

Though we live in Sri Lanka, we do not know the realities of the war. Restrictions on reporting from the war zone and self-censorship have denied us the truth. When 60,000 people die and 100,000 are made refugees, instead of showing emotion, we become cold and emotionless. In these circumstances, it is almost impossible to find any journalist who is sensitive to what is happening, and prepared to struggle to uplift the value of human dignity through his work. I see Nimalrajan as one of these rare human beings. His voice was silenced because it was a challenge to a society without a conscience. I have no doubt that the aim of his assassins was the unobstructed continuation of this society.

In the whole of the last 17 years, we have only seen a handful of creative works based on the war. It is frightening to see the number that fall into the category of shallow creations based on fantasies portraying ill-conceived, clichéd Utopias. My belief is that the false image created by the media is the inspiring force behind these 'works of art'.

Nimalrajan emerged as a unique force to fill this vacuum. With the war becoming more protracted, people began to suspect the authenticity of the information provided by the local media. The gap was filled by the BBC Sinhala service, whose coverage was enhanced by the reliable and authentic voice of Nimalrajan, who reported what was happening on the Jaffna peninsula.

In a deeply divided society that lives in constant suspicion, Sinhala and Tamil listeners grew to trust and believe Nimalrajan. Just as he was able to fill the vacuum in the Sri Lankan media, his death has created another vacuum. We need journalists who are not afraid to report what they see, regardless of the present hypocrisy. Without them, I do not see a future for Sri Lanka. ❏

Mylvaganam Nimalrajan, a freelance journalist with the BBC World Service and local Sinhala and Tamil publications, was murdered in Jaffna Town on 19 October by unidentified men suspected of links with the pro-government Eelam People's Democratic Party. This is an edited extract from the eulogy delivered by director **Prasanna Vithanage**, *whose award-winning anti-war film* Purasanda Kaluwar (Death on a Full Moon Day) *is banned in his home country* (Index 5/2000)

Lanka's 2000 Parliamentary Elections (European Union, Election Observer Project, October 2000, pp78); *Creating Peace In Sri Lanka: Civil War & Reconciliation*, edited by Robert I. Rotberg (Brookings Institution Press, 1999, pp218); *Government And The NGOs: an ambivalent relationship* by Peter Kloos (Vrije University, Amsterdam, 1999, pp42).

SUDAN

Osman Idris and **Dr Hassan Bashir**, journalists with the *Al hadaf* daily newspaper, the voice of the Arab Baath Party till the military coup of June 1989, have been arrested, it was reported on 24 October. *Al hadaf* resumed as an Internet publication recently, and Dr Bashir is the owner of the provider which hosts it. (IFJ)

SWAZILAND

On 13 and 14 October, several journalists trying to cover a story concerning the chieftancy dispute in the Macetjeni and Kamkhweli areas were harassed and detained. **Ginger Ginindza** from the Swaziland Televisions Authority (STA) was detained for four hours and the footage from his camera confiscated. News crews from the *Times of Swaziland* newspaper, led by journalist **Nimrod Mabuza**, were also harassed and prevented from covering the story. (MISA)

SYRIA

As part of the amnesty of 600 political prisoners, journalists **Samir al-Hassan** (*Index* 6/1994), and **Faraj Ahmed**

Birqdar (*Index* 3/1993, 1/1994, 2/1994, 6/1994, 3/1997, 4/1999) were released on 16 November, the 30th anniversary of the late Hafez al-Assad's takeover. Al-Hassan, Palestinian journalist of the weekly *Al Asifa* and publisher of the magazine *Fatah al-Intifada*, had been detained since April 1986. Birqdar, poet and contributor to the Lebanese monthly *Al-Tarik*, had been held since 1992. (RSF)

TANZANIA

Ally Saleh, the island-based correspondent for the BBC, has been accused of kidnapping two women by the Zanzibari authorities. Saleh denied the charge in court and has been released on bail. The prosecution is alleging that the kidnapping took place on 29 October, when two women were held against their will for three and a half hours. The journalist had interviewed the women in connection with a story for the BBC about election fraud and allegations that people were bussed in to fraudulently vote in other constituencies. (*MISA*)

TUNISIA

On 19 October **Moncef Marzouki**, head of the National Council of Civil Liberties, was prevented from boarding a flight to Barcelona where he was due to address a seminar on human rights abuses. He was brought before a magistrate, who levelled a number of accusations, including claims that he belonged to an 'unrecognisable association' and had 'distri-

buted tracts of a nature likely to disrupt public order'. Marzouki has faced sustained harassment from the Tunisian authorities in recent years (*Index* 3/1995). (International Federation for Human Rights) Copies of the weekly *Jeune Afrique-L'Intelligent* were impounded on 23 October by the authorities. The paper, printed in France, was seized at Tunis airport shortly after it had been unloaded from a flight. The authorities offered no explanation for the action, but it is thought that President Ben Ali took umbrage at a profile of human rights activist **Mohamed Talbi** that appeared in the issue. (RSF) **Taoufik Ben Brik**, a writer for the French newspaper *Le Croix*, was detained by security officials at Tunis airport on 22 November after returning from a conference in Europe. Although he was released after two hours, a number of books he was carrying were declared 'illegal imports' and confiscated. Ben Brik has faced continuous harassment from the authorities in recent years (*Index* 5/1998, 2/1999). (RSF)

TURKEY

Issue 61 of the weekly *Roja Teze* (New Day) (*Index* 5/2000) was confiscated on the orders of a State Security Court in September. A total of 32 issues, published in both Turkish and Kurdish, have been seized since the newspaper was founded. A Gaziantep-based newspaper *Firat'a Yasam* (Life on the Euphrates) has been banned indefinitely (*Index* 4/2000). (IMK)

The condition of blind Turkish writer–lawyer **Esber Yagmurdereli** (*Index* 2/1998, 4/1998, 6/1999, 3/2000), who has already spent 17 of his 55 years in prisons for crimes of opinion, is arousing increasing concern in international circles. On 13 October, 11 western NGOs sent a joint letter to Prime Minister Bulent Ecevit, asking him 'to immediately and unconditionally release Esber Yagmurdereli from prison'. (Cildekt)

The trial of a group of writers and journalists continued on 17 October. **Yavuz Onen**, **Husnu Ondul** (*Index* 1/2000), **Mehmet Atilla Maras**, **Yilmaz Ensaroglu** and **Salim Uslu** were charged for signing the booklet entitled *Freedom of Thought 2000*, which contains a banned book and 60 articles. (TIHV, Info-Turk)

The lawyers of the comic *Pine* (*Index* 4/2000), which is published in Kurdish, have applied to the European Court of Human Rights because the publication has been banned in the State of Emergency Region since 12 March. Lawyer **Cihan Aydin** stated that the name of the comic had changed seven times but the ban continued. (Yeni Gundem, Info-Turk)

On 23 October Istanbul State Security Court again charged **Akin Birdal**, (*Index* 4/1998, 5/1998, 1/1999, 4/1999, 5/1999, 6/1999, 1/2000, 2/2000, 3/2000, 6/2000) vice-president of the International Federation for Human Rights and former president of the Turkish Association for Human Rights for 'incitement to hatred'. Birdal was charged for his criticism of Turkey's

stance on the genocide of the Armenians. (Cildekt)

A documentary film, *The World's Back*, made by Spanish television and a number of Human Rights NGOs, won the Critics' Prize at the San Sebastian International Film Festival. The documentary outlines the life of **Leyla Zana** (*Index* 1/1997, 5/1998, 6/1998, 1/1999, 4/1999, 5/1999, 6/1999) and her husband **Mehdi Zana**, a former mayor of Diyarbekir who, after spending 17 years in Turkish prisons, now lives in exile in Sweden. The daily *Hurriyet* described the film as 'hostile to Turkey' and 'a second *Midnight Express*' after the well-known Hollywood film on Turkish prisons. (Cildekt)

The central offices of the journal *Yasadigimiz Vatan* (Our Native Land) were raided by police on 31 October. They broke down the doors and smashed the walls with a sledgehammer. The employees, together with around 30 others who came in when they heard the commotion, were detained. (*Cumhuriyet*, Info-Turk)

One thousand socialists demanded on 6 November that the government posthumously restore the citizenship of the **Nazim Hikmet**, who died in exile 37 years ago. Hikmet was a political prisoner in Turkey for 18 years. In 1959 he was stripped of his citizenship and died in Russia four years later. (BBC, Kurdish Media)

An Istanbul prosecutor has filed charges against the Kurdish Institute and its director, **Hasan Kaya**, on grounds that its existence is

'illegal'. The centre opened eight years ago and provides information on the survival and development of the Kurdish language. Hasan Kaya said that the charges had no legal basis and that the institute has participated in many meetings where high-level state officials had been present. (Yeni Gundem, Kurdistan Observer)

A court sentenced ten policemen to between five and ten years in jail for torturing teenagers arrested for putting up leftist political posters. The police had previously been acquitted twice on lack of evidence, but the Appeal Court overruled and ordered a retrial. Fourteen teenagers were arrested in 1995 for hanging political posters in Manisa. They were taken to a local police station and beaten, tortured with electric shocks, stripped naked and sexually abused. (Kurdish Media)

Cengiz Candar's weekly column in the mainstream daily *Sabah* has been withdrawn by the management on grounds that it 'insulted the military'. The column failed to appear on 4 November and, in its place, was a printed explanation that said it broke the law. The column had discussed evidence of a smear campaign by the military, named the Special Action Plan, aimed at discrediting prominent journalists and intellectuals – including Candar – by linking them to the banned Kurdistan Workers Party. The military had confirmed the existence of a document which outlined this plan, but claimed it was only a 'memo' containing suggestions. (*Cumhuriyet*)

Police shut down and sealed off the theatre of a Kurdish cultural centre on 19 November after a play in Kurdish was staged. The shutdown came after the mainstream paper *Hurriyet* reported that the Mesopotamian Culture Centre (MKM) was showing a Kurdish play. (Kurdistan Observer)

TURKMENISTAN

Nikolai Nikolaevich Gherasimov, a journalist for the Azerbaijan News Agency and a Turkmen national, was arrested on 7 November and is currently being detained in a prison in Krasnovodsk. No reason has been given for his arrest. (WAN, CJES, RSF)

UKRAINE

A decapitated corpse and a mutilated skull, thought to be the remains of Internet journalist **Georgy Gogadze**, were found close to Kiev in the Taraschanskyi region, it was reported on 28 November. Traces of past injuries on the body led colleagues to believe that the remains were those of Gogadze, who disappeared on 16 September. The 31-year-old journalist was founder and editor-in-chief of the Internet site *Pravda*, which is highly critical of the government. Prior to his disappearance Gogadze was interrogated several times by police in the context of a criminal investigation. (RSF, IFJ)

UNITED ARAB EMIRATES

In early September the Ministry of Information and Culture banned a number of scholars at UAE University from publishing their writings. They include: Professor **Said Abdullah Harib**, Vice-Chancellor for Community Services; Professor **Mohammed Abdulah al-Rukin**, Associate Dean of Faculty of Law; Professor **Abdulrazak Fal-Faris** of the Economics Department; Dr **Khalifa Ali al-Suwaidi**, Associate Vice-Chancellor; Dr **Ateeq Abdulazeez Jakkeh**, Department of Political Science; Dr **Abdulraheem Shaheen**, Department of Political Science, and Dr **Ibrahim Alshamsi**, Department of Information. **Abdulhameed Ahmed**, former associate editor-in-chief of the *Al-Bayan* daily, was also banned: 15 other writers have been affected. Newspapers are now required to obtain ministerial permission for any columnist wishing to write on a regular basis. The decisions mainly affect the UAE's only private newspaper, *Alkhaleej*. Several TV and radio programmes were also banned: *Mirror of Opinion* of Dubai TV, *Vision* of Abu Dhabi TV, several religious radio programmes and two programmes from Sharjah TV. A number of distinguished journalists were also fired from the Ministry of Information. There is no judicial review of the ministry's decisions. (HRW)

USA

A French journalist who made a satirical film about Saddam Hussein had a death threat pinned to the letterbox at his Hollywood home, his bins set on fire and his house daubed in red paint, it was reported on 3 November. The film, made by **Joel Soler**, included shots of Saddam throwing hand grenades in a country lake and lecturing his aides on how best to shower. He obtained access to the Iraqi leader by pretending to be filming the country's suffering under UN sanctions. The note said: 'In the name of God the merciful, the compassionate, burn the Satanic movie or you will be dead.' (BBC News)

A newspaper editor was fired for including in the entertainment section a photo of a singer in a jumper bearing the logo 'fuct', it was reported on 1 November. **Nora Garza** was dismissed from her post at the *Monitor*, a daily in McAllen, Texas, because her superiors deemed the logo 'obscene'. She said 'For one, it's not obscene language. Two, it's just silly.' (sonicnet)

It emerged in mid-November that the individual central to the debacle surrounding the result of the presidential election, John Ellis, is the first cousin of Republican candidate George W. Bush. Ellis, a journalist with Rupert Murdoch's Fox TV, hoped to beat the competition by being the first to announce the election result on the night of 7 November. The Fox news network was the first to call the outcome of the poll, even though the tally from Florida had yet to be officially confirmed. Democrats accused Ellis of breaking election rules by attempting to influence the result. (*Guardian*)

VIETNAM

Eight documents, released by the Centre for Religious

Freedom on 10 November, reveal government plans to nullify Christian movements. Blaming Christians for the end of eastern European communism, the documents forbid 'gather[ing] people to study religion', and listening to foreign religious broadcasts. Christians may be pressured to sign a pledge form showing they have renounced their faith. (Freedom House)

ZAMBIA

On 4 October Information Minister Newsted Zimba named a 13-member team, dominated by civil servants, to serve on the country's Film Censorship Board. The appointments, gazetted in April, have been criticised by two of the country's main journalism associations. (MISA)

The verdict in the trial of *Post* newspaper editor-in-chief **Fred M'membe** is expected on 21 December. M'embe is charged with espionage for publishing an article entitled 'Angola worries Zambia Army' (*Index* 3/1999, 5/2000). (MISA)

ZIMBABWE

On 18 October four journalists were dragged by soldiers from their vehicle, forced to lie on the ground and were kicked and severely beaten with wire whips and batons. The beatings stopped only after the soldiers seized film footage taken by them of victims of earlier beatings. The journalists were **Peter Maringisanwa** and **Vincent Murwira** of the South African Broadcasting Corporation,

Chris Mazivanaga and **Rob Cooper**, cameraman and photographer respectively for Associated Press. (MISA)

The editor of the state-owned daily *Herald*, **Bornwell Chakaodza**, was dismissed from his post on 17 October, effective from 31 October. It is believed his dismissal is due to his editorial stance of moving away from unquestioning support for the government. (MISA)

Journalists covering parliamentary proceedings have been asked to confine themselves to the press gallery and to stop interviewing members of parliament in the courtyard, the *Zimbabwe Independent* reported on 7 November. Journalists have also been barred from entering the parliament bar and interacting with the MPs. However, the chief whips of both the ruling ZANU-PF party and the opposition MDC denied that they had made the complaints which led to the ban. (MISA)

On 2 November Information Minister Jonathan Moyo threatened to charge the independent *Daily News*, the weekly *Standard* and their senior staff with criminal defamation. The minister warned that the government would soon amend press laws in order to silence the two papers 'once and for all'. Moyo's statement relates to articles in the two papers reporting that President Robert Mugabe had lost a US$400m lawsuit for human rights abuses filed against him in the United States. Both quoted sources saying that, because Mugabe did not respond to the suit, the plaintiffs had won by default. US

judicial sources told the government-owned *Herald* that there had been no ruling in the case, but that Mugabe's time to respond had expired. (CPJ)

On 12 November police and plain-clothes officers, believed to be members of the Central Intelligence Organisation, seized copies of the latest album by singer **Oliver Mtukudzi** from market vendors in Harare and Chitungwiza. Mtukudzi's latest cassette has caused a stir because of its political, topical content. (*Standard*)

On 16 November the High Court ordered police to return equipment, excluding the transmitter, which was seized from Capital Radio on 6 October (*Index* 6/2000), after the station went on air without a government-allocated frequency. Under new regulations, it is illegal to possess a transmitter without a broadcasting licence. (MISA)

Compiled by: Andrew Barsoum, Gbenga Oduntan, Shifa Rahman, Polly Rossdale (Africa); Ben Carrdus, Louise Finer, Anna Lloyd, Jessica Smith-Rohrberg (Asia); William Escofet, Polly Rossdale (south and central America); David Gelber, Gill Newsham, Neil Sammonds, (Middle East); Humfrey Hunter (north America and Pacific); Louise Finer (UK and western Europe); Louise Finer, Katy Sheppard (eastern Europe and the Balkans).

Africa's first world war

Why is Africa, with all its challenges of economic and social development, embroiled in wars that threaten to engulf most of the continent?

ALEX DE WAAL

Brute causes

Why is there war in Africa? Many academic reputations have been built and ruined on a wide range of arguments about the supposed 'root causes' of violent conflict on the African continent. Some argue that wars were stirred up by the superpowers during their cold war confrontation; others that the end of the cold war saw a rash of 'new wars', an outcome of the geopolitical vacuum of the 1990s. There are those who argue that Africa's unequal incorporation into the world economy has systematically provoked violence; while others contend that Africa's neglect and marginalisation in the globalised economy have created war. Some claim that resource scarcity drives Africans to violence; others again that African wars are fuelled by the income from valuable resources such as oil and diamonds. Ethnic divisions, religious divides, the legacy of colonially created rivalries, weak or collapsing states, overblown 'winner-take-all' states, foreign meddling, lack of international interest – all are cited as causes of war.

Many eminent Africans, both scholars and policymakers, tend to subscribe to these views in their public statements and published analyses. What has happened, we may ask, to what is perhaps the commonest theory of war propounded by historians of Europe: that wars arise from the (mis)calculations of interest by political leaders? Niall Fergusson, concluding his epic *The Pity of War*, writes: 'The First World War . . . was nothing less than the greatest *error* of modern history.' Gabriel Kolko, in *Century of War*, attributes European wars to the self-delusions of political leaders who believed they could control and in a meaningful sense 'win' a war.

A parallel with Europe in the first half of the 20th century may not be inappropriate for contemporary Africa. Our hypothesis, 'War is started by men who mistakenly believe that they can control it and benefit from it', is so simple and obvious that it has usually been forwarded only by those who study far-gone times, or whose innocence of the dirty realities of politics leaves them the most honest – but the least influential – observers.

All history indicates that war, once started, cannot be controlled and can rarely, in any meaningful sense, be 'won'. Sober analysis of the history of wars would lead any political leader straight and without any qualification to the conclusion that it is a reckless gamble with the future of nations, classes, communities, even entire continents; that in almost any war of the last 100 years or so, not fought between hopelessly mismatched adversaries or blessed with extraordinary luck, the winners (if any) have been the bystanders. It follows that any leader who decides to go to war must be extraordinarily stupid or deluded. Given that most leaders are at least clever enough to rise to power, and not (yet) senile enough to become incapable of mastering the basics of staying in charge, we must ask, what delusions have captivated them?

The most important delusion is that past victory is a guide to the future. Unfortunately, the rare past instances of 'victory' have so captivated the imaginations of men (and, less often, women) that very many leaders harbour secret desires to repeat these fantastic, mythical feats. For those leaders who have themselves taken power by 'victory', this illusion is all the stronger. Indeed, by definition, a military leader in charge of a state has a successful experience of the use of violence in his personal history. Some are indeed masters of the military art. But this is a dangerous art to master, because its practitioners have a tendency to want to demonstrate their skills, and therefore rush to violent conflict while others may hold back. They become prisoners of their successes. Some are victorious less through their own brilliance than through the exhaustion or incompetence of their adversaries. (Left-wing militarists are apt to forget Lenin's dictum that the primary contradiction is internal – the chief skill demanded of the revolutionary strategist is knowing when to strike.)

But, given the human tendency towards giving a coherent narrative to the chaotic and inexplicable, opponents' mistakes become one's own successes. During the struggle, the slogan 'victory is inevitable' starts as a morale booster. Should victory occur, by skill, tenacity and a big dose of good fortune, its inevitability is falsely projected back into the past. And the victorious general believes that he has somehow grasped the magic formula of perpetual victory that has eluded every military commander in history including Alexander and Napoleon.

A second delusion is that machismo is a virtue. A strutting conceited militarism may help mobilise confused youth. Stubbornness and a pig-headed readiness to persist in the face of disaster may help bring some leaders to power. This can be a dangerous combination when it comes to making a judgement about the use of force. This is a step beyond hegemonic masculinity. This is militarism elevated to ideology – in rightist, leftist and other variants. It is the cult of machismo.

And the third delusion is that war is in some sense controllable and predictable. In this era of the supposed 'revolution in military affairs', Clausewitz is regarded as somewhat passé. His dictum that 'war is the conduct of politics by other means' is no longer considered applicable in a post-realist world where sovereign states no longer act in pursuit of calculable interest. But strip away Clausewitz's Metternichean theory of international relations, and his insights into military affairs hold as true today as in the days of Bismarck. War tends to the absolute – it is escalated, prolonged, jacked up in every way imaginable. Three-quarters of war is incalculable – 'friction', luck and the unforeseen are the main determinants of the outcome. These still hold true. Tens of thousands of young people can die in an inter-state war that began as a minor tiff over a disputed border area scarcely big enough to be a cemetery for the war's fatalities. A dispute over soldiers' pay or the posting of a battalion to another part of the country can spark a civil war that destroys a generation. A conflict over allocation of government posts can end up generating ethnic or religious extremism that completely alters the political landscape of a country. The causes of conflict in Sudan, Angola, Sierra Leone, and between Eritrea and Ethiopia are all real. But are they causes enough for full-scale war?

So why does a political leader start a war? Does there come a point at which a military leader is so fatigued by the demands of politics and diplomacy that he just closes his eyes and says, 'Fuck this political/ diplomatic process. It's too slow and too difficult and I don't have the patience or the skill in handling professional advisers and diplomats and all that crap. Let's just have a battle and kill some people and sort it all out.' Probably, yes. Probably, he feels either a surge of emotion ('gotcha!') or a sense of relief that at last he has delivered his (and his country's) future back into the hands of fate. At least he's been decisive.

The debris of war, 2000: prisoners in Zaire.
Credit: © Jenny Matthews / Network

He can sleep. The adrenalin flows.

And then a process of moral decay sets in. Human life becomes relative. The logic of war takes over: famously it becomes the statesman's master, not his slave. The demand of winning, or avoiding defeat, rules all. Politics, life, emotion, the calculus of means and ends, enters an alternative universe. This is the world of Macbeth: 'To mine own good all causes shall give way.' The longer or more bloody the conflict becomes, the higher the stakes, and the harder to give way: 'I am in blood stepp'd in so far that . . . returning were as tedious as go o'er.' Battles that slaughter thousands of sons, lovers, husbands, brothers become 'rounds'. Mass rape of girls and women, looting of towns and villages, burning of the essential foodcrops of farmers, become 'operations.' Some commanders cease to grieve over their dead comrades – these are the ones who thrive, winning promotion. They cease to have the normal, decent human virtues of consideration, discussion, tolerance. War breeds war. Militarism breeds militarism: decisiveness, command, orders, discipline, conformity.

The exhilaration of decision, the orgiastic delight of sending young men to their deaths, becomes the weariness of entrapment in a maze of confusion and hopelessness. The delusional thinking that sparked the initiation of the war becomes compounded, reinforced, locked into the demands of continuing at any cost. The decision to go to war in the first place was so fundamentally irrational that any peace settlement can only expose the flawed decision-making and debased values of the man who made it. Above all, war does not solve the problem that sparked it. At best it brings other problems, at worst a host of new problems, far harder to resolve. As starting the war was probably a cop-out from addressing tricky problems, how is the initiator of the war going to explain that, after a peace settlement, everyone has to go back to conducting messy

Kinshasa, Zaire, May 1997: Kabila's troops arrive in the capital.
Credit: © Chris Brown / Saba / Network

and uncertain politics at square one, or square minus one, or maybe square minus two hundred and fifty?

(One of the mediator's jobs may be to peddle the illusion, to the war's originators, that the settlement will be 'comprehensive' and 'once for all'. That way at least the commanders may stop the killing and give a pause for a return to the normal give-and-take of civilian politics. But there is an ever-present danger that our general – who was, to begin with, somewhat vulnerable to self-delusion – will actually believe that a peace treaty means the end of politics, and may shout 'betrayal!' when he realises that he has to negotiate, or face elections, or deal with dissent. Instead he may prefer to return to the comfortable familiarity of fighting on. 'Victory is just around the corner!' he will promise, again and again, as he drifts off into a fantasy world of perpetual fighting.)

War incubates extremism. War, especially protracted and costly war, demands a narrative of comparable scope and grandeur to make it meaningful, to keep its initiators in power, and keep their legitimacy over their people. Nothing justifies genocide, but it is a historic reality that genocidal extremism in Rwanda developed *after* the RPF invaded in 1990. The Southern Sudanese have legitimate claims to self-determination and deep-seated historical grievances. But Islamic extremism exploded and took power in Khartoum *after* the SPLA launched its rebellion. Similarly, Southern separatism and anti-Islamic sentiment have grown massively after the national Islamic coup. Eritrean nationalism was nourished in the crucible of the thirty years' struggle against Ethiopia. True, each of these tendencies had roots in the societies concerned. But history shows that using violence to repress a political movement is more likely to feed it than strangle it.

And in Africa, where the weaponry for battlefield escalation may be too expensive, and the bureaucratic machinery for mass conscription too ineffectual, our warmakers must resort to ideological escalation instead. Ethnic or religious extremism is a poor country's Panzer Brigade, and its leader's political Viagra – a way of sparking into life the paralytic centralism that afflicts a militarised regime with no war to fight.

Extremism is a god-sent cop-out for war leaders – both those who espouse the extremist cause and those who oppose it. Extremism neatly leapfrogs this awkward issue of individual moral responsibility and decision-making. The discourse of inevitability takes charge. This is the real epistemologic comfort zone for our war-initiators. The necessity for war becomes easy to explain, while peace becomes a safely remote possibility.

War is a golden opportunity for corruption. War is an expensive business, and if the frontline commanders can finance it from their entrepreneurial activities so much the better. Most war-fighting, in any case, consists of soldiers sitting around, drinking, playing cards and sexually abusing women. Few African militaries can afford to pay pensions or support families. The opportunity to earn enough cash to buy a small hotel or a nice car replaces the more standard benefits laid on for soldiers from industrialised countries. Ministries of finance, closely scrutinised by the IMF, like to keep as much 'defence' expenditure off the national accounts as they can. The World Bank and the IMF have a history of disliking semi-official military–commercial linkages (they tried to close down Sudan's 'Military Economic Corporations'). Better to fight your war where there may be diamonds, gold, timber or, at the very minimum, enough hungry people to draw international relief agencies.

Take an ordinary, fairly inefficient, cash-strapped African economy with a small army and a significant but basically benign informal sector. It is just about managing to balance the books and achieve modest growth under some pretty adverse international circumstances. Introduce war: a civil conflict or a foreign adventure. The government simply cannot square the circle of funding destruction and death. Pressures that the country might have withstood with minor hardship (a drought, a hike in the oil price, a fall in the price of its main export), suddenly become disasters. The wheels of patronage can no longer be greased. Instead, there is inflation, currency depreciation, banking scandals, a crime spree, thuggery in high places. Ministerial and private bank accounts may be raided. A reputable officer sent to sort out reports of front-line misappropriation may be found dead.

As much in response to this crisis of legitimacy and smooth functioning of government as in response to the war itself, the security men move into the real positions of power in the president's office. Tight-lipped, arrogant, certain of their exclusive control of the logic of the national interest, the securitat take on the role of gatekeeper to the big man. Decision-making becomes more centralised, more secretive, more informal. The power meetings take place at midnight. The security men and a few trusted confidantes echo back to the boss what they well know he wants to hear. Contrary information is filtered out. Contrary opinions become not just dissent but treason. The calculus of national interest becomes a psychological game between the war leaders, each isolated with a coterie of advisers, each less and less able to feel the pulse of the national sentiment, each less and less able to make the imaginative leap necessary to understand the predicament of the other. Whole countries become hostage to these idiosyncratic, impenetrable, highly personalised apparatuses of power.

Our terminology begins to break down. What language do we have for the men who start wars? 'Warmonger', 'aggressor' and their cognates are all terms that are founded on an implied distinction between legitimate and illegitimate wars. This distinction is not entirely without value – it is important to distinguish between a war-initiator who deliberately provokes a violent conflict with a peaceable neighbour or who plunges a peaceful country into turmoil, and the one who responds. But few cases are so clear-cut, and in most cases it is *both* leaders who conspire together in turning a dispute into a war. Moreover, every war-initiator pleads provocation, usually with some justification. And even the 'victim' of the initial war-move, once he has adopted the logic of violent conflict, may then become the one who escalates it, turning a minor conflict into an all-out war. The first will then complain: 'It all started when he hit me (back).' Likewise, the terminology for those who sustain wars is impoverished. 'Warlord' is inadequate. 'Commander' has too much legitimacy. How about, 'self-deluded *macho* militarist, drunk in charge of an army and/or sovereign state'? Maybe we should settle for 'warmaker' for now.

Wars generate wars. While almost every citizen and soldier becomes weary of war and dreams of how to find a way of getting some leverage on the warmakers, those in charge derive power, wealth, legitimacy and pyschological satisfaction from the state of affairs. Peace for them is a problem. A rebel commander who may at best hope for the post-war position of vice-president can enjoy the de facto status of a head of state: red carpets, meetings with senior ministers and heads of state, international conferences. He can keep a European foreign minister waiting – and he doesn't need to publish his accounts . . .

The central dilemma in peacemaking is that peace has to made between the warmakers, deluded thugs that they are. But satisfying the demands of the warmakers can only leave a country in a deeply vulnerable position: ruled by people for whom personality, ideology, constituency and history give them a dangerous proclivity to start fighting once again. Some of the dangers can be overcome by thorough programmes of disarmament and demobilisation and the reintegration of former soldiers into civilian life. But the longer-term challenge is the demilitarisation of politics: creating an environment in which the use of force for political ends no longer commands any legitimacy.

Africa's world war is the continent's biggest mistake. It is in the hands of Africa's leaders to stop it. ❏

Alex de Waal *is the director of Justice Africa*

COLETTE BRAEKMAN

One disaster after another

One day, when the guns fall silent, the world will conclude that the population of the Congo has been the victim of a gross haemorrhage of human lives. By then, in the face of media indifference, it will be too late

For 30 years now, Father Carlos has been living in Bumba, in the heart of Equator Province of Congo, an area that was once the breadbasket for the entire country and used to supply Kinshasa. Nowadays, there is no river traffic because of the war, so shopkeepers cross more than a thousand kilometres of jungle by bicycle to go and fetch salt from Kisangani. The priest is an acute social observer and does not disguise his concern. He has noticed that the population is shrinking; he is registering more deaths than births. He can show you the proof: for one thing, they are taking away the doors and the benches from his school to make them into coffins. He also stresses that, for the first time since the arrival of the missionaries at the beginning of this century, attendance at religious services has taken a dramatic plunge. It is not that the faithful have suddenly lost their faith, the reason is more down to earth: 'My parishioners have nothing to wear, their clothes are in rags; they're just afraid to come out; they're ashamed,' says the priest.

In Equator Province, which is controlled by the rebel leader Jean-Pierre Bemba, but also in Kivu, where another rebel group, the Rassemblement Congolais pour la Démocratie (RCD), sponsored by Uganda and Rwanda, operates, and in Kisangani, observers without exception confirm Father Carlos's fears: the population *is* shrinking. Because vaccination is not happening and there is no health care, major endemic diseases such as sleeping sickness, river blindness and measles

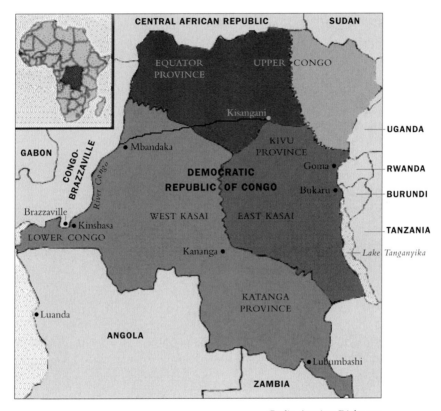

Credit: American Diplomacy

 Government controlled

 Rally for Congolese Democracy (RCD) controlled

 Movement for the Liberation of Congo (MLC) controlled

MLC/RCD controlled

have surfaced again. All over the country, armed groups are holding
farmers to ransom, raping their wives, forcing civilians to flee into the
bush and destroying health centres and dispensaries. A survey conducted
by the US NGO International Rescue Committee (IRC), which tried
to catalogue the human suffering caused by the war, came to the
conclusion that in the five Congo provinces, 2.3 million Congolese
had been killed between August 1998 and May 2000, and that the
deaths of another 1.7 million were a direct result of the war.

How do you start to explain the silence surrounding this conflict in
which six national armies and 18 armed groups are taking part? How
do you explain the fact that the Congolese people, in every part of the
country, continue to state categorically that this is not *their* war? How
do you explain the denials that it has anything to do with a partition
of the country when the facts make this ever more obviously the case?

Difficulties in gaining access to the area are not the whole story.
Journalists have to overcome multiple obstacles, but if they do manage
to get through these, there's no shortage of material. The Congolese are
unanimously of the view that everything must be done to bring the war
to an end. But the feeling that the press is turning away from the Congo
because the powers that be are allowing a country in the heart of Africa
– a veritable treasure chest – to be looted and torn apart without a word
being said, is widespread.

Unearthing the origins of the Congo disaster means turning back
a decade. In central Africa, the early 1990s were marked by
two major events: in what was still Zaire, the power of the man who
had been the region's guiding light, its godfather, was on the wane.
Mobutu Sésé Seko, an ally of the West during the Cold War, was
coming to the end of his power and being forced to allow a multiparty system and a sovereign national congress. From 1990 onwards,
he had had to face sanctions including the withdrawal of all foreign
co-operation and aid.

As for neighbouring Rwanda, Tutsi exiles who had taken refuge in
Uganda had set up a political and military group, known as the Rwanda

DRC, 1999: boy soldiers recruited by rebels train with sticks in Lisala.
Credit: © Jenny Matthews / Network

Patriotic Front (RPF) that aimed to overthrow the Habyarimana regime which, for 30 years had maintained Hutu supremacy in Rwanda. Rwanda, Zaire and Burundi all found themselves facing the challenge of democratisation, the appearance of multiparty systems and the fact that competing political forces were exploiting ethnic loyalties, group solidarity and hatred of anyone different to win a populist power base.

It was the two smaller countries in the Great Lakes region that would trigger the crisis. In Burundi, President Ndadaye, the first Hutu to be democratically elected head of state, was assassinated in October 1993 by a group of Tutsi military. His killing had consequences in neighbouring Rwanda where the Habyarimana regime had just concluded an agreement to share power with the RPF. The putsch in Burundi increased the mistrust felt by the Hutu extremists in Rwanda, and President Habyarimana's clan privately reneged on power-sharing. It began methodical preparations for genocide: this included training Interahamwe militia to kill '1,000 Tutsis every 20 minutes', purchasing a million machetes and psychological propaganda diffused via Radio Mille Collines. The attack on Habyarimana's aircraft on 6 April 1994 was the starting signal for the slaughter which had been planned long in advance. Three months later, when the RPF arrived in Kigali and seized power, the final act of the tragedy was played out: 800,000 Tutsis and moderate Hutus were massacred and, fearing RPF reprisals, more than two million Hutu civilians fled to neighbouring countries. One and a half million stayed in huge refugee camps in Kivu Province, near the Rwandese frontier. At that stage, instead of responding to the genocide, which it had been powerless to prevent, instead of trying to bring aid and stability to a Rwanda that lay in ruins, the international community was concerned only with the humanitarian problem represented by the refugees. The camps, which were maintained by dozens of NGOs, became centres of hatred: they were taken over by extremists involved in the genocide and transformed into military bases where the next stage of the conflict was planned. In addition, the enormous numbers of refugees and the international aid they attracted destabilised Kivu, a province already overpopulated and where the delicate ethnic balance was easily exploited by local politicians. The only beneficiary of the situation was the Mobutu regime, supported by France with its dream of revenge by its Hutu allies.

The Rwandese strongman, Paul Kagame, had long been predicting that, if the international community did nothing to disarm the security

Kinshasa, Zaire, 1994: rummaging through rubbish. Credit: Ed Kashi / Network

threat in the camps, he would take the initiative himself. In September 1996 he did just that. An army made up of Congolese Tutsis – known as the Banyamulenge – Lumumbist rebels and a majority of Rwandese and Ugandan shock-troops crossed the Kivu frontier. These troops, under the banner of the AFDL (Alliance of Congolese Forces for Democracy and Liberation) with Laurent-Désiré Kabila, once part of Patrice Lumumba's defeated opposition in the 1960s, as their leader, were to carry out a twofold mission. They were to dismantle the refugee camps by force, compelling the civilians to go back to their own country, and to pursue the military and the militia responsible for the genocide through the Congolese jungle and eventually, once they had got as far as Kinshasa, to overthrow the Mobutu regime.

Kinshasa, Zaire, May 1997: Kabila's troops arrive in the capital.
Credit: © Chris Brown / Saba / Network

Once again, on 17 May 1997, when Mobutu fled, betrayed by his army which had scarcely fought at all, the world got it wrong. Everyone was delighted to see the end of Mobutu's dictatorship and congratulated Kabila on having set up what was now to be the Democratic Republic of Congo. There was talk of an 'African Renaissance', of 'new African leaders' who had united to rid the world of an old-fashioned dictator.

In reality, the overthrow of Mobutu and Kabila's seizure of power had been made possible by a most unusual alliance. As well as the armies of Rwanda and Uganda, which had decided to intervene in Zaire for reasons of national security, other powers had also intervened. From January 1997 onwards, Angola joined the alliance and Zimbabwe made financial contributions to the operation. Angola's governing MPLA

(Popular Movement for the Liberation of Angola) had old scores to settle with Mobutu who, for years, had given shelter and support to Jonas Savimbi's UNITA, a rebel army which had kept the country at war continuously since its independence in 1975. By fighting alongside the AFDL, Angola hoped to cut Savimbi off from his base and finally ensure military victory. Zimbabwe, well aware of the strategic position of the Congo, of the potential 50 million market for its own burgeoning industry and of its enormous mineral resources, envisaged lucrative co-operation between African countries.

The euphoria of the first few days after the liberation of Kinshasa was short-lived. The Congolese political forces that had fought from inside against the Mobutu dictatorship were quick to realise that the new regime was tightly controlled by its foreign allies. Etienne Tshisekedi, the leader of the opposition to Mobutu, was already claiming in May 1997 that Kabila looked more like a hostage than a president. It is true that the new president is surrounded by Congolese Tutsis who are politically close to the Kigali government and that, without an army, he is dependent on foreign armies. The new Congolese army chief of staff is James Kabarebe, one of Kagame's closest deputies.

The new regime's first year in power was fraught with contradictions of this kind. To claim to be president of all the Congolese, Kabila had to pay a 'debt of ingratitude' to his allies. This meant he gradually distanced himself from his earlier advisers and insisted on surrounding himself with ideological fellow-travellers (people who, like himself, were former members of the Lumumbist resistance) and members of his ethnic group, the Lubas of Katanga Province.

Under pressure from his allies and a prisoner of his own ideology, Kabila showed himself incapable of listening to the political forces of the nation which had fought for a true democracy, not for a people's republic. Their disappointed guaranteed an attempt to overthrow the man who had failed them. This disappointment was shared by Canadian- and US-owned mining companies that, in return for mining concessions, had made financial contributions to the war. Once Kabila was in power, he set about revising or even denouncing such contracts. He refused either to repay the 'war-loan' given by Rwanda and Uganda or to repay the US$14 billion debt contracted by the Mobutu regime, which, he said, had brought no benefits to the people.

Opinions are divided on Kabila's first year in power. On the first anniversary of the new government, the international press was unanimous in claiming that 'he had made a complete mess of it' (*Libération*, May 1998). But inside the Congo, that year is regarded as something of a golden age: government employees were paid for the first time in many a month; the launch of the new currency, the Congolese franc, was successful; and the entire country, buoyed up with hope, had gone back to work without waiting for international aid to materialise.

Aid was waiting on the outcome of a UN commission investigating the killing of Hutu refugees, something the regime was anxious to avoid since it had no desire to allow responsibility to fall where it belonged: with the Rwandese commandos whose task had been to hunt down their genocidal enemies. In July and August 1998, the situation came to a head: Kabila became aware of an assassination plot against him and decided to dismiss his Tutsi advisers and to send back the Rwandese military who were providing the command-structure of his army. While this decision was well received by the Congolese people, it led Rwanda and Uganda to play their cards: the RCD, supported by their armies, appeared in Goma and Bukavu. Rwandese troops and Congolese units, stationed in Kivu Province by Rwandese 'military advisers', rapidly seized a huge area in the east of the country while the Ugandans, who were subsequently to support two other rebel movements, occupied the northern regions, the eastern province (Kisangani) and Equator Province.

While everyone was waiting for a new group to take over in Kinshasa, Kabila was crafty enough to appeal to other allies: he persuaded Angola, and more especially Zimbabwe and Namibia, to come to his assistance. An offensive against Kinshasa by the Rwandese and Ugandan armies was prevented at the last minute by the intervention of Zimbabwe and Angola. Meanwhile, the regime was stirring up popular resistance in the capital and calling on the population to hunt down Tutsi infiltrators – a form of resistance which looked very much like an anti-Tutsi pogrom.

Since August 1998, the Congo has been struggling with the consequences of a putsch that failed. The Lusaka peace agreements, so laboriously concluded in July 1999, show no sign of being implemented. This is because they attempt to deal with several quite different issues and because the declared intentions of the belligerents mask carefully hidden agendas.

The first matter on the Lusaka agenda is the democratisation of the country and good government. With this in mind, the agreements allow for a dialogue between all the Congolese forces. Such a dialogue was not only meant to involve all internal political forces but was also supposed to place Kabila on an equal footing with the rebel fighters who were presented as the voice of a popular uprising. Time has passed its verdict on this claim: in the regions which they control, the unpopularity of the rebel movements, themselves internally divided, is evident; they are regarded as nothing more than an expression of Ugandan and Rwandese intentions.

The second matter, one which is of concern to the international community, is the security of the Congo's frontiers, especially those with Rwanda and Uganda. In the first year of the Kabila regime, the frontier provinces of Rwanda had been ravaged by armed incursions carried out from Kivu by Hutu extremists. Up to now, the presence of Rwandese and Ugandan troops in the Congo has been justified by the need to pursue hostile groups, referred to as 'negative forces', in particular the remaining members of the Interahamwe, the group responsible for the Rwandese genocide. Hostility to the Kabila regime is also being justified by the fact that Kigali is claiming that the Congolese president has incorporated Rwandese and Burundian Hutu rebels into his army.

As time goes by, however, and in the face of the real concerns behind the fighting, such security concerns are becoming less and less plausible. It has emerged that in the frontier areas of Kivu Province the Rwandese army and its RCD allies are doing nothing to improve the security situation; they are not fighting the armed groups which systematically attack dispensaries, schools and parish buildings, and force the inhabitants to flee into the bush. They are, instead, directing their military efforts more to the south, towards Katanga and Kasai provinces.

The Ugandan army, meanwhile, is doing nothing to pursue its ADF (Allied Democratic Front) opponents, but it is known that senior Ugandan officers, such as Brigadier James Kazini, act as a cover for lucrative dealings in gold, coffee and precious woods. In the areas where Rwandese troops are operating, rare and precious minerals such as columbium tantalite (coltan), cassiterite, niobium and tantalum find their way towards Kigali (no export taxes paid, of course) and the region's resources are being systematically looted. Even the money produced by the numerous and crippling local taxes disappears in the direction of the neighbouring countries.

On the government side, Zimbabwe's participation is also largely financed by resources from the Congo. Zimbabwean industrialists have interests in copper and cobalt from Lubumbashi and Kabila is paying for his allies' war effort with diamonds from the Mbuji Mayi region. As the war continues, we begin to see what is really at stake. The countries bordering on the Congo, perhaps at the instigation of western mining interests or of political groups which do not support Kabila, are making less effort to respond to the need for security than to ensure that they have a worthwhile income by dipping into the country's mineral wealth, its gold, but most of all its diamonds.

In addition to this, in Rwanda's case, there is the not unfounded suspicion that it intends to expand economically, demographically and militarily in the direction of Kivu Province; it was only the arrival of first the German and then the Belgian colonists that stopped the westward expansion of the last independent kings of Rwanda, the Mwami, Rwabugiri and Musinga.

As for the West, despite the declarations of principle upholding the territorial integrity of the Congo and the inviolability of its frontiers, despite all the pious pledges, what we see is, if not actual indifference, then at least inaction. No country so far has offered to participate in the UN force that was provided for in the Lusaka accords and no international finance for it has been forthcoming. Countries such as Rwanda and Uganda which could be seen under international law as aggressors, have not been subjected to any kind of sanction. Even after the Rwandese and Ugandan forces fought at Kisangani in June 2000, in the course of a six-day war in which 6,500 shells fell in the working-class areas, killing and wounding thousands of the civilian population, no sanction, no demand for any kind of reparation was imposed on the belligerents. So far all attempts at mediation have been in vain, and it is noticeable how the Congo war is dividing Africa into opposing camps: English-speaking Africa, the countries aligned with the USA (except for Zimbabwe and Namibia), support the rebels; francophone countries, fearful of some sort of explosion, support the central power in the person of Kabila. Even the presence of the facilitator, Dr Quett

Masire, former president of Botswana, who is after all considered to be one of the wise men of Africa, has become a complicating factor. He wants to apply the letter of the law of the Lusaka accords and consider Kabila as simply a representative of one of the factions on the ground not as a recognised head of state. Consequently, Kinshasa rejects him as an arbitrator. The democratic deficit of the regime is an additional obstacle because it, too, lends support to the pretexts for the war.

In fact, the current situation in the Congo is reminiscent of that in the 1960s when the West objected to the prime minister, Patrice Lumumba, and encouraged the secession of Katanga and Kasai provinces to weaken the central power. Later, when Mobutu, the friend of the West was safely in power, the provinces were rapidly brought back into the Congo.

Today, when the priority is to bring down Kabila, who is considered to be uncontrollable, the idea of a de facto partition of the country does not seem to worry western powers. But one day the country's humanitarian problems may force us to recall even darker days in its history: the terrible years of the Congo Free State when Leopold II and his henchmen did everything they could to open up the Congo basin to international trade and when the population were cowed, dispossessed and plundered to the point where their only means of escape from forced labour was to run away and hide and die in the bush. That was Joseph Conrad's *Heart of Darkness*. ❑

Colette Braekman *is a journalist with* Le Soir, *Brussels, and a regular visitor to* DRC

DEMOCRATIC REPUBLIC OF CONGO COALITION

Democratic Republic of Congo 150,000 soldiers from the Congolese Armed Forces (FAC), of which only 25,000 are fully trained. Most of the FAC's weapons are Chinese, and the force suffers a debilitating shortage of vehicles. The FAC controls the railway network and most of the country's airfields, both of which have escaped heavy bombardment.

Interahamwe militia 40,000 Hutu rebels, exiled from Rwanda and largely in refugee camps. The group was responsible for prosecuting the 1994 genocide in which 800,000 Tutsis and moderate Hutu perished. The Interahamwe is based in the Kivu Province bordering Rwanda in the hope of renewing an offensive against Rwandese Tutsis.

Zimbabwe 11,000 soldiers from the Zimbabwe National Army. Once considered an irresistible force on the battlefield, the force's reputation has dwindled in recent years. Nevertheless, the Zimbabwean presence has significantly improved the profile of President Kabila's military coalition, although Robert Mugabe's government has been effectively bankrupted by the conflict.

Angola 3,000 soldiers from the Angolan army were deployed initially, along with a considerable air-force presence. Since October 2000, the number of Angolan troops in the Congo has fallen steadily. They have annexed many of the oil installations in western Congo and it is unclear whether the Luanda government will relinquish them at the request of Kabila.

Namibia 4,000 troops deployed initially, half of whom were withdrawn in late 1999. The remaining Namibians operate alongside Zimbabwean troops. Public opinion is largely opposed to the war, and there is anger at President Sam Nujoma's unilateral decision to join the conflict.

Chad Sent 1,000 soldiers in September 1998, all of whom were withdrawn 15 months later. Poorly trained, the Chadian forces wreaked havoc in northern Congo, peddling their weapons and pillaging local communities.

Libya Colonel Muammer Qaddafi has offered only moral support to President Kabila, but sees involvement in the conflict as a way of reintegrating the DRC into the international community.

Sudan Not directly involved in the conflict, but the Sudanese government has sent financial aid to Ugandan rebels allied with Kabila.

ANTI-KABILA OPPOSITION

Rwanda 15,000 soldiers from the Rwandese armed forces. Rwanda supported Kabila's bid for power in 1997 but, alarmed by the growing entente between the Congo and extremist Hutu groups, the Tutsi-led Rwandese have now declared war on Kabila. The Rwandese are hoping to profit from resources in the north Kivu region.

Uganda Of the 16,000 soldiers sent initially by President Yoweri Museveni, only 5,000 remain in the Congo, fighting a guerrilla campaign. The poorly equipped Ugandans suffered heavy losses at the hands of Zimbabwe special forces early on in the struggle and have since clashed with the Rwandese over control of the diamond trade.

Burundi 1,000 soldiers, mainly Tutsis. Burundi's involvment in the conflict is limited, with operations largely confined to exercises against Hutu militias near Lake Tanganyika and to securing the border with the DRC.

Rally for Congolese Democracy (RCD) A coalition of disaffected Congolese rebel groups. The RCD has an army of 50,000, comprised mainly of dissident FAC soldiers who broke away under Major Ondekane in 1998. The RCD is led by a number of Mobutu's and Kabila's ex-colleagues, including Bizima Karaha, former minister of foreign affairs, and Moise Nyarugabo, once private secretary to Kabila.

Movement for the Liberation of Congo (MLC) 10,000 rebel soldiers, trained by the Ugandan army. The MLC was founded in November 1998 by businessman Jean-Pierre Bemba, formerly an aide to Mobutu. It opposes Kabila's 'dicatatorial rule'.

Banyamulenge soldiers A Tutsi–Rwandese contingent of the FAC until they were dismissed by Kabila in 1998 as part of his drive to rid the country of its foreign military presence. The Banyamulenge soldiers are fighting to have their right to Congolese nationality accepted by Kabila and their alliance with the Rwandese forces has, therefore, been uneasy. ❏

*Compiled by **David Gelber**, principally from information supplied by Michael Quintana*

BERNARD TABAIRE

Counting the cost

How many Ugandan soldiers are deployed in the Democratic Republic of the Congo? How many of those have been killed since the outbreak of the Congo war on 2 August 1998? How many injured? How many taken prisoner? How much money does Uganda spend on the war? Where does that money come from? And why is Uganda there at all? The Ugandan government remains silent and the people keep up their questioning

Uganda claims it deployed troops in the Congo to prevent a genocide of the Banyamulenge that President Laurent Kabila was about to unleash on them for their alleged support of Rwanda, which had sought to overthrow him in 1998. Kampala's involvement also aims to prevent Sudan supporting the Allied Democratic Forces (ADF), an Islamic fundamentalist group that has terrorised western Uganda for four years from bases inside the DRC. The Sudanese support the ADF, as well as Joseph Kony's Lord's Resistance Army in northern Uganda, in retaliation for Uganda's support for John Garang's rebel SPLA in southern Sudan. It has been fighting the Khartoum government for the last 20 years.

'The ADF is no longer able to get supplies from Kabila or the Sudanese,' said President Yoweri Museveni in a May interview with the UN Nairobi-based Integrated Regional Information Network. 'So our Congo mission has been partially accomplished.'

Ugandans attribute their army's failure to secure the western border, where the ADF remain active, to its getting mired in other people's affairs thousands of miles inside Congo. The Ugandan leadership is silent on whether it succeeded in stopping a genocide; meanwhile, estimates claim that the nine countries embroiled in that war have together lost more than 100,000 soldiers and civilians. United Nations' estimates in September put the number of displaced at 1.8 million.

Experts say that having lost their political and military objective in

Uganda, 2000: war as lottery. Credit: © Mike Goldwater / Network

the Congo, the Ugandan forces (UPDF) have resorted to plundering that country's abundant timber, gold, diamonds, coffee and other resources. In March, the Uganda government-owned newspaper, *New Vision*, reported that the UPDF was stealing four-wheel-drive cars from Ugandans, loading them on to suspicious cargo planes at the Old Airport in Entebbe under heavy military guard, selling them in the Congo and returning with tons of timber, coffee and other merchandise. The army denied the accusations and threatened to sue the paper. In the end, it didn't, but it was not lost on Ugandans that in September 1998, a plane (whose manifest at Entebbe International Airport bore forged names and destination), carrying a senior UPDF officer, Colonel Jet Mwebaze, crashed in western Uganda near the Congo border. The crash killed Mwebaze and revealed more than US$1 million in cash stashed aboard the plane. Other passengers included Israeli businessman Zeev Shif, a partner in general Salim Saleh's Efforte Corporation. Knowledgeable circles contend that the plane was on a regular gun and gold/diamond run to and from the Congo.

Saleh, Museveni's younger brother and a hero of the 1981–86 bush war, has been named in almost all major national scandals of recent years but has never been prosecuted. The scandals range from getting a kickback of US$800,000 (to which he confessed) in the 1998 purchase of junk helicopters from Belarus that cost the country US$6 million, to the dubious purchase of the country's biggest commercial bank in which US$100 million went down the tubes. Under the holding company Calebs International, Saleh's business concerns extend to air travel, mining, coffee, security, etc.

The more serious aspect of all this, however, is that a network of looting generals and other security elements in East and Central Africa have developed a stranglehold over the region's governments. No president can move against any general and hope to survive. To hold on to power, regional presidents turn a blind eye to the looting.

'Hogwash,' says Museveni dismissively of claims that his army are soldiers of fortune. But the UN is sufficiently convinced to set up an investigative panel. It met Museveni on 18 November.

The clashes between the UPDF and the Rwandese army (RPA) in Kisangani in August 1999 and May and June 2000 marked a fallling out of comrades and convinced Ugandans there was no need for their country's continued stay in Congo. The clashes, supposedly over control of diamond and gold mines, left Kisangani in ruins and mask strategic differences and the countries' support for rival rebel groups.

In September 1999, one year after the war started, a *New Vision* poll showed that 81% of Kampala residents wanted the UPDF out of Congo. In August 2000, 4,000 of the estimated 11,000 Ugandan troops were withdrawn. But the popular feeling persists that the government has been less than transparent in its Congo dealings. Neither parliament nor the military top brass was consulted.

Nor have Ugandans any idea how many of their compatriots have been killed, injured or taken prisoner. Close Congo-watchers such as Charles Onyango-Obbo, the influential editor of the independent Kampala daily *Monitor*, says estimates put the dead at 1,000. Member of parliament Aggrey Awori, who recently visited the DRC, says he met 143 UPDF POWs held by Kabila, a figure disputed by the army, which claims 'only one Ugandan' is held prisoner.

In the end, however, it is the effect of the war on the economy that most rankles Ugandans. They attribute the steady depreciation of the shilling since 1998 to resources being diverted to the war. Ministry of Finance and IMF officials disagree. 'The fall in the Ugandan shilling is simply a corrective response to the balance of payments shocks; that is, the lower world price of coffee and the higher world price for petroleum,' wrote Dr Zia Ebrahim-Zadeh, IMF Resident Representative in Uganda, in the *Monitor* on 11 November. But if the exploitation of Congo's minerals was used to finance the war rather than lining officers' pockets, goes the popular reasoning, the economy would be sound and the government would not need to raid national reserves.

The independent media are prevented from investigating the Congo adventure. Onyango-Obbo says that while *New Vision* journalists are free to enter Congo, *Monitor* journalists must be accompanied.

What drives Museveni is a persistent belief in pan-Africanism, nurtured while he was still a student in the late 1960s, and his aspiration to lead that movement. 'I support an East African political federation, so that East African countries, Rwanda and Burundi are together,' said Museveni in May last year. 'Later, Congolese leaders and freedom fighters can be approached so that an East and Central African political union can be a reality. This arrangement would solve the question of bad politics, insecurity and markets.' ❑

Bernard Tabaire *was formerly an editor with the* Monitor. *He is currently studying in the US*

GRANT FERRETT

What are we fighting for?

Zimbabwe's involvement in the war in Congo is draining the country's economy and President Mugabe has precious little to show for it

Farai spent much of last year living in hostels in and around London, doing odd jobs in an effort to scrape an existence. Two years ago he was a highly trained signalman in the Zimbabwean air force with more than a decade's experience and a career ahead of him. A six-month tour of duty in the Democratic Republic of the Congo (DRC) was enough to persuade him that he'd be better off trying his luck as an illegal immigrant, 6,000 miles from his wife and child, rather than risk getting killed like his colleagues in a war he did not believe in.

'It's Mugabe's war and we were there as part of a private army,' says Farai. 'We were being killed because of Mugabe's personal pride. I had one good friend and three close workmates who died there. And for what? It's not a war the soldiers believe in.'

Such bitterness is shared by many Zimbabweans, who have watched the economy disintegrate while the government continues to pour money into a conflict few support. A recent opinion poll by the Johannesburg-based Helen Suzman Foundation suggested that just 15% of the population supported continued involvement in the war.

'The people were very angry two years ago, before they realised the damage it would do to the economy. Now they see things collapsing all around,' says John Makumbe, a lecturer at the University of Zimbabwe. The war has not only helped to drain what little foreign currency Zimbabwe has left, it has also used up scarce supplies of diesel as convoys of tankers head north across the Zambian border on the long journey to Zimbabwean forces in the DRC. It has also helped to undermine any

Harare, Zimbabwe, 2000: peace rally. Credit: © Peter Jordan / Network

remnants of investor confidence as the government resorts to printing
money, thus fuelling inflation, in order to pay for the war.

The precise cost remains largely unknown. The government simply
refuses to disclose how many soldiers have been killed or injured,
describing such information as 'sensitive'. Little more is known about
the economic impact. Finance Minister Simba Makoni told parliament
in August that the first two years of military involvement in the DRC
had cost 10 billion Zimbabwean dollars (c. US$200 million), a figure
widely assumed to be a gross understatement. A draft government
document leaked to the International Monetary Fund indicated that the
true cost was around US$1 million a day, putting the total cost to date at
more than US$800 million, or four times the entire health budget for
the coming year.

The government appears unconcerned. 'You don't consider the economy before you deploy a military force,' says Defence Minister Moven Mahachi. 'We are defending the sovereign legitimacy of a fellow African state. Surely our economy shouldn't be the barometer of whether we help or not?'

Contrary to Mahachi, Zimbabweans like Otilia believe charity begins at home: 'The government has got no money because it's paying for soldiers in the DRC. So long as Mugabe goes on sending troops up there, it will be difficult for us. He just doesn't care about the people.'

Otilia is an HIV and Aids counsellor. She has watched many of those she has worked with die slowly in their homes, without any medication apart from paracetamol. Families often no longer have the money to pay for the removal of the body, much less for a funeral. Yet such is Otilia's mistrust of the government, she does not believe a new tax intended to create an Aids support fund will have any significant effect while the war continues. 'The Aids levy won't be used for people with Aids,' she says. 'It will go to the DRC.'

Given that the war is clearly so unpopular, why does President Mugabe insist on maintaining about one-third of his armed forces in a country with which Zimbabwe shares no common border or historical connection? Makumbe believes the president has become too deeply involved to countenance the unilateral withdrawal of Zimbabwean troops, regardless of the cost to his country: 'He's just boosting his own ego. The president began by playing an obsolete game of thinking that if he got involved in a war, that would boost his image among the people. Now he can't get out without losing face.'

Yet it would seem that any initial hopes among the Zimbabwean elite of making large sums of money in Congo, largely through diamond mining, have proved groundless. Mahachi has publicly admitted that joint ventures set up between the Zimbabwean defence forces and their Congolese counterparts to help finance the war have produced nothing. A prominent Zimbabwean businessman, Billy Rautenbach, lost his position as head of the Congolese state-run mining company, Gécamines, a year after taking over.

Moreover, President Kabila has shown an increasing unwillingness to toe the Mugabe line, repeatedly failing to turn up for talks aimed at resolving the conflict. While Makoni tells parliament that the cost of the war is unsustainable, his fellow minister Mahachi gives no indication when Zimbabwe's forces will be pulled out. 'We averted a possible catastrophe in Kinshasa, but instead of the world thanking us, they have called us names,' laments Mahachi. 'At least the people of the DRC appreciate us. They tell me, "Please help us to repel these aggressors." They shout, "Viva Zimbabwe!" I always come back from there rejuvenated.'

Back in Britain, Farai has begun a nursing course. His wife is currently with him, but their young son remains in Zimbabwe. Far from the repression which has become a hallmark of his home country in recent years under President Mugabe, he feels more free to speak about the war and the president. 'Mugabe fought for democracy during the war of liberation [in the 1970s], but he's changed. He has run out of ideas and become arrogant. He has nothing to offer but conflict.' ❏

Grant Ferrett *is the BBC correspondent in Zimbabwe*

Above
*New houses are built for those
returning from Zaire, 1997.*
Credit: © Jenny Matthews / Network

Left
*Near the Ugandan border, 1980s:
women fetching water rest
on their way home.*
Credit: © Mike Goldwater / Network

Facing page
Women and children farming.
Credit: © Mike Goldwater / Network

Another one down?

In the wake of presidential elections from which all but one of the
main contenders was banned, and again in the run-up to parliamentary
elections, Africa's current wave of violence arrived in Côte d'Ivoire – an
unlikely destination, but one where the conflict looks unlikely to find a
quick resolution. A human rights organisation in Paris is investigating
the slaughter of 57 young men whose bodies were found scattered near
woodland at Yopougon, a northern suburb of Abidjan, in the wake of
flawed presidential elections. The victims were allegedly stripped and shot
by police on 26 and 27 October. They were identified as sympathisers of
Alassane Ouattara, a former prime minister excluded by a Supreme Court
ruling from the presidential election because of doubts over his Ivorian
nationality – he has links with Burkina Faso.

Ouattara's power base is among Muslim northerners and the families
of those who migrated into Côte d'Ivoire to work on the plantation crops
– the country is a world leader in cocoa – that made the country wealthy
by African standards and Abidjan a byword for sophistication and urban
comfort.

The presidential election held on 22 October was fought primarily
between a military coup-maker, General Robert Gueï, who had ousted
the civilian administration on 24 December 1999, and the only significant
political leader not excluded, the Socialist Party's Laurent Gbagbo. When
Gueï tried to steal the election, the Abidjan public took their cue from
the recent action in Belgrade that forced Yugoslav's President Slobodan
Milosevic to yield power: with the help of southern Christian support,
they swept Gbagbo into the presidency.

The Yopougon youths died apparently because they did not share the
same political or religious beliefs as their neighbours and the prevailing
authorities. It should be said that the scale of this tragic moment is trivial in
comparison with ethnic cleansing in the Balkans in recent decades – when,
at the extreme, thousands of civilians could be put to death within a few
days for being of the wrong faith.

Yopougon is symptomatic of a deeper malaise that cuts through much
of Africa but is by no means exclusive to the continent. The countries of

Africa are subject to multiple cleavages inherited from the centuries of European intervention that have left them enfeebled and fragile, with extraverted economies, dysfunctional political systems and conflictual societies.

It is ahistorical to suggest that the African is afflicted with some inherent vice: the history of every society and culture includes phases of conduct later deemed to be vicious and shameful by the society itself. It is likewise ahistorical to ignore the great fault-line along which so many countries lie, particularly in West and Central Africa. The rival inroads of Islam and Christianity have a differential impact within the colonially imposed boundaries of many of the countries where the internal conflict that was anomalous in the 1960s has recently become a norm. Sierra Leone and Liberia with their admixture of returned slaves forming elites have suffered some of the greatest upheaval.

The religious differences are a shorthand for differing traditions of cultural and educational practice that encourage or discourage access to economic opportunity and advancement. Sometimes ethnicity and religion are coterminous. The scramble between competitors is accelerated when there are tight constraints on resources. Africa's poverty grinds harder and harder through the familiar worsening of terms of trade, ecological pressures and substitution for the export crops on which the colonial economies were predicated. Paradoxically, new sources of wealth from mineral extraction – oil finds in Nigeria and Sudan, conflict diamonds in Sierra Leone and Angola – can exacerbate societal divisions or generate new agents of plunder.

The conflicts in West Africa are not so much new phenomena as re-enactments of unequal power relationships in new forms. Nor are they likely to be of a temporary character. Among domestic and international (bilateral or multilateral) players, it is hard to point to any significant corrective agent.

Where are the effective proponents of food self-sufficiency, production for domestic needs, education for genuine rather than rhetorical self-reliance? The comprador elements and the international institutions profit from the subordinate role Africa continues to play in the world system. Even the call for delinking that was being made in the 1980s has been overtaken by technological changes in communications that outleap natural barriers. The perpetrators and the recipients of violence are now just another facet of globalisation. ❏

Michael Wolfers is a London-based Africa specialist

VICTORIA BRITTAIN

Myths of Congo

From a simple scenario of the triumphant ousting of one of Africa's most notorious tyrants, Mobutu Sésé Seko, by a coalition of the continent's more respected leaders, the war in Congo has become a war of spoils and horrendous brutality

The fragmented, shifting alliances of rebel groups in eastern and northern Democratic Republic of Congo (DRC) make them frightening and dangerous places to work. Information is patchy and unreliable. Myth and rumour have become the common currency of aid agencies, diplomats and journalists. Today's myths about who is to blame for the continuing war and the persistent attacks on civilians are as misleading as those which four years ago forecast the remaking of the continent on the back of the new Congo led by President Laurent-Désiré Kabila.

The central issue today is the disarming of two groups of genocidal killers whose leaders should be behind bars awaiting trial for crimes against humanity. One is the Hutu militia who perpetrated the 1994 genocide in Rwanda and are now part of the army of Kabila, trained and led by the Zimbabwean army. The second is the Unita fighters in Angola who still control by terror large parts of the Angolan countryside.

The first group received critical support from France during Operation Turquoise in 1994 when French soldiers created a safe area for *génocidaires* in southern Rwanda as the Rwanda Patriotic Front swept to power. They were then looked after by the UN and aid agencies for two years while they prepared a second genocide. The second group was made an effective fighting force by apartheid South Africa with US funds and the complicity of Zaire in the 1980s. Unita's leader, Jonas Savimbi, was supported by the CIA as late as the elections of 1992.

Both the RPF government in Rwanda and the governing Popular Movement for the Liberation of Angola (MPLA) in Angola have serious security problems created by outsiders and linked to DRC. This is the key dynamic of the war for these two important actors, not, as myth has it, lucrative business in DRC's minerals.

August 1998 brought these former allies, Rwanda and Angola, on to opposing sides, myth has kept them there and done much to prolong the war. Central to this myth was the conviction of part of the Angolan leadership that Rwanda was working with Unita. By July 1998, both Angola and Rwanda were completely disillusioned with their former protégé Kabila. Both were involved in training his army, and Rwandese officers provided his personal security and his chief of staff. Their wish to see him replaced by someone more serious was an open secret.

The tension erupted when Kabila unceremoniously dismissed the Rwandese military and in an astonishing betrayal began to recruit their enemies, the *génocidaires*, not only in DRC, but in UN refugee camps in Congo-Brazzaville and Central African Republic. He even sent his son, with the son of Idi Amin, the former Ugandan dictator, to Juba in southern Sudan where they recruited former Amin soldiers.

Then, in August 1998, three companies of Kabila's army rebelled in Kinshasa, many of them Banyamulenge from eastern Congo, and 100 were killed. The others fled, made radio contact with Kigali, and Rwandese troops were dispatched to help them. Five thousand former Mobutu soldiers in training at the base of Kitona also mutinied. Kabila looked close to falling, but was saved by the Angolans and Zimbabweans moving in with aircraft and tanks. A second group of Rwandese soldiers under Colonel James Kabarebe, formerly Kabila's chief of staff, flew into an extremely confused situation. Angolan intelligence had been kept informed by their allies, the Rwandese, of what they were doing, but old personal links between individuals in Kabila's cabinet and some of the Angolan leadership from the MPLA days as a liberation movement brought them down on his side. Kabarebe saved his men by taking them – by agreement with both Unita and MPLA – through a Unita-controlled zone where a Rwandese plane withdrew all of them.

The incident became mythologised – not least by Unita officials who had every reason to know better – as a military alliance between Rwanda and Unita. On the back of this myth grew another one, swallowed initially by UN officials researching Ambassador Robert

Fowler's report into Unita's diamond smuggling: the Rwandese leadership was dealing diamonds with Savimbi. Apologies were made privately to Rwanda by western officials for the error, but the damaging story is still repeated.

The 15,000 to 20,000 *génocidaires* in Kabila's army are the first key to peace. Without them he could not continue the war. And the terror myth that keeps them in DRC is wearing out for the men, if not their leaders. Day after day, wary, defeated men trickle over the border and give themselves up, having heard, they say, that reconciliation in Rwanda is real. It can only remain real when the political class in DRC creates — for the first time since independence — internal stability, rather than external destabilisation. It will never happen with Kabila in power. ❏

Victoria Brittain is deputy foreign editor at the Guardian, *London*

Culture

'My daughter was kidnapped when she was six months pregnant. I know she had a boy. I am looking for him.'

Grandmothers of the Plaza de Mayo

A play in Buenos Aires is based on testimonies from the Mothers and Grandmothers of the Plaza de Mayo
p168

A Tibetan exile tells of Chinese efforts to destroy his language and culture
p176

Zhide Dratsang, near Lhasa, 1991: ruined statue.
Credit: © John Miles / Tibet Images

PATRICIA ZANGARO

A propos of doubt

D oes memory grow or fade with the passage of the years? The ageing
individual may argue that the clarity of recollection declines. Societies,
however, have usually experienced the reverse. Time placates fear; changing
circumstances in the law and in government help draw out forgotten scenes. New
generations want to know, and demand that their elders produce accounts of the
hidden age. In Argentina, the youngsters, the children of the 'disappeared' (that
word which the military dictators of the 1970s contributed to the language), the
eldest aged about 25, the youngest not yet 20, have become the most militant
seekers of memory. They call it their 'search for identity'.

Former president General Jorge Rafael Videla, who seized power in March
1976 after overthrowing the weak and corrupt government of Mrs María Estela
Perón, widow of the late general, is recorded on film telling an interviewer that
the 'disappeared' do not exist, they simply are people who 'are not here any
more'. He waves his arms, demonstrating that the hidden captives 'disappeared'
into thin air. It was a key statement in military policy: it represented the
censorship of memory, a ban on identity.

The military fell in 1983, largely due to their defeat in the Falklands/
Malvinas war in June 1982. In 1985, the members of the military junta were
tried and sentenced for crimes against humanity. In 1990, they received a pardon.
It had a clause that excluded possible charges for abduction of children. Eight
years later, on 9 June 1998, a court placed Videla under house arrest on charges
of aiding the abduction of babies, born to mothers in captivity, who 'disappeared'.
The babies were often given up for adoption; their mothers murdered. Some of
those babies have now grown up, and want to know who they are.

This is not unique to Argentina, of course. Gitta Sereny, in The German
Trauma: Experiences and Reflections 1938–1999 (Penguin 2000) exposes
'forgotten or misunderstood episodes, like the Nazis' systematic abduction of
Aryan-looking children of families in eastern Europe and giving them to German
parents'. In Argentina, too, the babies of blonde mothers were the most sought-
after prizes.

Buenos Aires, Argentina: in the Plaza de Mayo

The 'Mothers of Plaza de Mayo', who have won high-profile international recognition, began the search back in 1976, when they were forced to queue in the square in front of Government House to await information they would never be given. They still march in Plaza de Mayo, every Thursday, at 3pm, to continue their campaign for information about the young men and women who were 'disappeared' in the 1970s for their opposition to the military regime. The military say the information was destroyed in 1983. But some files have been found. Some of the mothers have formed the 'Grandmothers of Plaza de Mayo', to search not just for their children, but for the grandchildren that some of the women were carrying when they were abducted and who are known to have been born in captivity.

In 1999, the story of the 'Grandmothers' was told in Searching for Life: The Grandmothers of the Plaza de Mayo and the Disappeared Children of Argentina *by Argentine-born Rita Arditti (University of California Press). A Spanish imprint based in Buenos Aires has issued the book in translation.*

The children of the 'disappeared' have themselves formed HIJOS ('children'), to campaign for their identity and to identify the torturers and killers of the 1970s. One of their public demonstrations is a play, compiled from the accounts of Grandmothers and HIJOS. From a low-profile opening in June 2000, on a university stage, the play transferred to a commercial theatre and ran through October 2000. It has also been distributed on film.

The question put from the stage to the audience is, 'Who are you?' 'Do you know who you are?' 'Are you sure that the name you have been given is really yours?' A propos of doubt (A propósito de la duda) *is produced under the rubric Theatre for Identity and aims to bring history to young people. The cast is a mix of professional actors, members of HIJOS and students.*

Andrew Graham-Yooll *is senior editor at the* Buenos Aires Herald *and former editor of* Index

A PROPOS OF DOUBT

Actors assemble on darkened stage. SPOTLIGHT on BOY bouncing a ball. Sound of helicopter overhead. The BOY leaves the ball and walks off.

A GRANDMOTHER picks up the ball, and shows it to two others who look on in distress. SPOTLIGHT on a couple of 'APPROPRIATORS' – the name given to the adoptive parents of a child of a 'disappeared'. Seated on chairs a MAN and a BALD YOUTH who wears headphones connected to a Walkman. A WOMAN stands behind the BALD YOUTH vigorously massaging his head.

GRANDMOTHER I (*Wondering*) Is baldness hereditary?
GRANDMOTHER II (*Thoughtful*) Baldness . . . is hereditary . . .
GRANDMOTHER III (*Vehement*) Baldness is hereditary.
   MALE APPROPRIATOR laughs.
THREE GRANDMOTHERS Baldness is hereditary!
MALE APPROPRIATOR My son is certain we are his parents. We have the documents, they are all in order. I do not need to go for any tests. To prove what? We are not going to be judged here. We are condemned in advance. Appropriators, torturers, repressors. That's what they say we are. I ask you if you see any sign of torture in the boy? All I know is that I have worked all my life as a policeman. I told the boy never to say his father was a policeman. That is not lying. It is omission. Nobody lies in this house. Today, in Argentina, those of us who fought for our country are criminals. I think that I, and many more, deserve a monument instead of persecution. But putting aside the monument bit, they should at least leave us in peace. Not me, a soldier struggling against ignominy, but these poor innocents. They suffer the most. The family is being destroyed. Unfortunately, human rights belong to the Left. We are not human. We have no rights.
GRANDMOTHER I For as long as there is a single person with their identity stolen . . .
FEMALE APPROPRIATOR (*Interrupting*) They want to take him from me! They talk about identity. And what about all the years he has lived with me? Eh? Is he going to be born again? If there is anybody who is innocent in this situation, it is my son. And now they want to condemn him to exile. I am and always will be the mother. I brought up a healthy son. I have to care for the physical and mental health of my son. I am

not going to allow them to sicken him with hatred and resentment. Do you want me to read the letter he wrote to me when he was ten years old?

MALE APPROPRIATOR (*Uncomfortable, whispers in her ear*) Not now. This isn't the right time.

FEMALE APPROPRIATOR (*Who has already unfolded a piece of paper and has put on her reading glasses*)

'Mother most courageous,
Who cares for me with love,
You are the most beautiful rose
Who spares me from pain.
When at night I wake
From my sad nightmares
You cure my wounds
With your love sincere.
Do not walk out of my life,
Mother dear, I love you!'

THREE GRANDMOTHERS For as long as there is a single person with their identity stolen and forged, the identity of all is in doubt.

FEMALE APPROPRIATOR embraces the BALD YOUTH.

BALD YOUTH I was lucky. I have a family, a career, a car. I feel like Number One. I am great with the women. Just like my Dad. He says that when he was in the force he shagged them all. The only thing that screws me is my baldness. My Dad, the old dog, has hair coming out of his ears. But when he was young he was bald, just like me . . . (*Stops, confused*) I was lucky. When I get my degree my Dad promised to give me a hair implant. He doesn't like baldies. He says they look like faggots, that he feels like grabbing them, and busting their balls. My mother, just in case, spends her time massaging my head. Better hairy than with busted balls, like my Dad . . . (*Stops, confused*) I was lucky. When my hair grows I'll be just like my Dad. I am going to fuck everything. I am going to run right over the world. I am going to grab all the baldies, and bust their balls. I don't like baldies. They are just like my Dad . . .

He stops, concerned by the accusing look of the APPROPRIATOR.

YOUNG WOMAN I (*Approaches him and whispers*) It is not the same to belong to a place as to look as if you do.

BALD YOUTH looks at her.

YOUNG WOMAN I My mother said, 'Give me the fork.' It was a film of a family birthday. She was there for a second, and said, 'Give me the fork.' My mother was eight months pregnant when they took her. I was born in Pozo de Banfield [a notorious detention camp first identified in the report *Never Again (Nunca Mas)* published in English by *Index* in 1986]. A policewoman appropriated me. I must have rewound the film 20 times. My mother, all the time, said, 'Give me the fork. Give me the fork.' It's the only image I have of her alive. I never wanted to see the policewoman again, not even to swear at her. If somebody lies to you about something so basic, which is who you are, where you come from . . . How can you not doubt every word she says? Deep down you know. It is not the same to belong to a place as to look as if you do. I love to go on Sundays to my grandparents to eat pasta. My uncles go there, so do

Buenos Aires, 2000: performance by Theatre for Identity

my cousins. Every time I say, 'Give me the fork,' I laugh. I don't know, it is as if I feel that my mother is there. Not her absence, her presence.

Sound of the helicopter returns. The YOUNG WOMAN runs off. The THREE GRANDMOTHERS approach the APPROPRIATORS, who retreat, indignant.

GRANDMOTHER I My daughter was kidnapped when she was six months pregnant. I know she had a boy. I am looking for him.

GRANDMOTHER II My three children disappeared. Graciela, the youngest, was about to give birth. I have no information on any of them.

GRANDMOTHER III My daughter-in-law was pregnant when she was abducted with my son Ignacio. I was told that a girl was born at the Military Hospital. I am still looking for her.

A MAN in the stalls starts shouting.

MAN Just a minute! I cannot keep quiet. I have something to say. When the coup happened I had just finished my border guard training. We were confined to barracks and then I was transferred to Mobile Unit I at Campo de Mayo [military barracks], which was a detachment trained to fight guerrillas. I was assigned to several groups, in the city and outside the capital. I was in the Olimpo Brigade [a notorious detention centre, later used in the film *Garage Olimpo*]. My job was to drive the prisoners. I transported them from one place to another, or to the Metropolitan Airport, or to Ezeiza Airport. I drove a truck sto . . . (*he looks around*) . . . stolen from the Bruckman Brothers family, just like all the unit's vehicles. The prisoners were heavily sedated, unconscious, sometimes delirious. On the last journey I had to take a woman who was about to give birth. I was never told what was going to happen to the prisoners, but one could imagine it. I saw several pregnant women at Olimpo. I took one captured woman to the military hospital, and that was where an intelligence officer took charge of the child. It was a way of protecting them, so that they would not grow up in a subversive atmosphere. The mother was dead. She was taken back to the base, and from there to Puente Doce, where the bodies were cremated in large vats. Tyres were thrown in, and then petrol, then the body was thrown in, and then more tyres. I feel no weight on my conscience because I never killed anybody. I only transported the prisoners.

A group of youths assembles and starts a surprise and noisy escrache, *a demonstration to identify and draw attention to the* MAN. *They shout 'Murderer! Assassin!'*

The BALD YOUTH *begins to walk off, but the* BOY *intercepts him.*

BOY I was torn from my parents' arms. My grandmother is still searching for me.

CHORUS OF YOUTH (*To the sound of the drums beating in the* escrache – *the drums are traditionally used in the carnival* murgas, *and have been adopted in most political demos*) And you, who then are you? You, do you know who you are?

YOUNG WOMAN II (*Going to face BALD YOUTH*) My brother has just had his 20th birthday. I am still looking for him. I had imagined him as a little nuisance with whom I would some day be able to play. It's hard to believe that we will never have what we did not share, what we did not say to each other.

GRANDMOTHER I It is not just the voice of the blood calling.

GRANDMOTHER II It is the call of the soul.

GRANDMOTHER III It is the voice of my daughter who demands that I find my grandchildren.

CHORUS OF YOUTH You, do you know who you are?

YOUNG MAN I (*Going to the BALD YOUTH*) I only recently learned the story of my life. The cloudy memories were because I was five years old the day they took my parents, my uncles and my grandparents. They left my brother and me in the park holding our toys. The memories are a blur, but we have memories.

CHORUS OF YOUTH You, do you know who you are?

BOY The most important thing is to know who you are. Everybody has to know who they are, if not they are nobody, or think they are someone else.

YOUNG WOMAN IV I wonder how long the appropriators think they can go on cheating us?

YOUNG MAN II (*To the BALD YOUTH*) I want to know if I have a brother. I dream of him, a little brother who is 22 years old. I need him because he is a part of who I am. What hurts is not just the doubt, but the lies.

GRANDMOTHER I am 70 years old, and I have been searching for 20. The love for our missing kin is what drives us. Not knowing where one has come from is like floating in the air, without any roots.

CHORUS OF YOUTH You, do you know who you are?

BOY My granny is looking for me. Help her to find me.

    BALD YOUTH begins to leave, looking very disturbed.

YOUNG MAN III (*Calling after the BALD YOUTH*) Baldy! They say I have the same way of crossing my arms. Like this. As if I was cradling a child. My father disappeared when I was four years old. My family said that he had gone to Tierra del Fuego. But I don't look like him. That's what they say. But I think I have something of his at the edge of my mouth. Like this, like a smile. Can you imagine what it means to have your own family lying to you? Of course, you can't see these things in photographs I would like to know how he held his cigarette, how he went for a crap, if he liked eating sardines. Even if they lie to you, deep down you know. Some mornings when I wake up I don't know why I have such a strong desire to eat sardines . . . Frozen. That's how my father looks. Frozen in a photograph as a kid. But he was a living person, wasn't he? He may have had a nervous tic in his mouth, like a smile. Maybe he ate sardines,

Buenos Aires, 2000: members of the production team for
A propos of doubt *– including grandmothers – watch rehearsals*

like I do. It would be wonderful if the photo suddenly started moving. If it started to talk, or laugh, or swear, or just say a lot of stupid things. He might cross his arms, as if he was cradling a child, like this, just like me. And you, who are you?

CHORUS OF YOUTH You, do you know who you are?

GRANDMOTHER II In 20 years none of us will be alive, but the search will go on for all those who have doubts about being the children of a lost generation.

GRANDMOTHER I Every person we find is as if we had found our own grandchild.

YOUNG WOMAN IV (*Walking towards the BALD YOUTH, she is heavily pregnant*) Torture during pregnancy, parturition in captivity, separation from the mother shortly after birth . . . That is written in some part of the soul. I hope that some day, now or in 40 years, my brother will start searching.

CHORUS OF YOUTH You, do you know who you are?

Drums and chorus louder and louder.
Blackout. ❏

Patricia Zangaro's *script was based on statements by the Grandmothers of Plaza de Mayo. Directed by Daniel Fanego. First presented 5 June 2000 at Rojas Theatre (University of Buenos Aires). First English-language publication in* Index. *Translated by Andrew Graham-Yooll*

PEMA BHUM

Mao's cuckoo

A Tibetan remembers the Cultural Revolution and how students found a way of circumventing its all-embracing censorship

Before the Cultural Revolution, Chinese official publishing houses produced a number of modern-format books. To be sure, these included many revolutionary titles, but they also published several Tibetan cultural and literary classics. Later, with the denunciation of Tibetan culture and literature as 'superstitious' and 'old thought', these earlier works were banned. In 1971, major reforms were made in Tibetan grammar. From then on, even revolutionary texts were not allowed to have the traditional Tibetan punctuation *dbu-khyud*, marking the start of a passage, nor the *shad*, signalling the end of a phrase.

One day between 1970 and 1972, while I was still at Malho Nationality Teachers Training School, I went outside to find a sunny spot behind our classroom to read. I had brought with me a revolutionary book written in Tibetan. One of our Tibetan teachers, Dorje Tsomo, was already seated there reading a Chinese book. She was a relative of the scholar Sungrab Gyamtso who was in prison then for being a 'cow's-demon and snake-spirit'. So that she herself would not be infected with 'the poison of old thought', our teacher had broken off all contact with her senior relatives, including her mother and father.

I opened my book and began to read.

'Pema Bhum,' she said. 'You are young. Your mind is fresh. Reading old books like this will harm your brain.' Her eyes were kind as she spoke these words to me.

'This is the story of the heroine Liu Hulan.' I showed her the book. The book was about a 14-year-old girl who during the War of Resistance against Japan had been stabbed to death by enemies of the Communists. Mao Zedong himself had praised her saying, 'Glorious in life, she died an honourable death.'

After looking at the front and back cover of the book, my teacher said: 'You're right. This is the story of Liu Hulan. But look at this . . . and this.' She gestured to the *dbu-khyud* preceding the book title and the double *shad* after the title.

'Uhm.' I didn't know what to say. Though I had seen these punctuation marks before, I hadn't known what they were called. It was also the first time I'd ever heard they weren't allowed.

'This is a *dbu-khyud* and that is a *shad*. They are in all the superstitious books. They are not allowed, however, in revolutionary books. I am going to show this book to our school officials. If they say it is all right to read, I will return it to you.' She took the book and walked away. Several days passed. I never did hear if that book was allowed or not, but I never saw it again.

Eventually, almost any book published before the Cultural Revolution – regardless of its content, format or publisher, and even if it was published when the Chinese Communists first came – was banned.

With the practice of copying *la-gzhas* (traditional love songs banned during the Cultural Revolution but secretly collected and copied by hand to circulate as a form of *samizdat*) now ended, another clandestine copying project began at our school. The books were spelling and grammar texts published before the Cultural Revolution, modern editions of works by past scholars and present-day scholars now in prison. Since these teachers were now considered 'cow's-demons and snake-spirits' and their works were 'poisonous weeds', we lent such books to each other and copied them surreptitiously. Though there were many copies of these books at first, they later became hard to find. Most people would make their own replicas from other people's hand-written copies. The three most popular were Tseten Zhabdrung's *Tibetan Grammar Treatise*, Akhu Sungrab Gyamtso's *The Essence of Sum-cu-pa*, and *Spelling: Ray of Sunlight* (*Gangs-can-gyi sgra-rig-pa'I bstan-bcos, Sum-cu pa'i snying-po, Dag-yig nyi-ma'I 'od-zer*).

Most students didn't have money to buy notebooks for copying such texts. Rather, they would buy plain white paper and make their own books, the only option they could afford. During the morning breaks at school, students would return to their rooms and close their doors and windows. Sometimes they would pretend that no one was inside, by having a friend lock the door from the outside. Only then did they set to work: cutting the sheets of paper, sewing the bindings and ruling the paper to make their notebooks.

Though most students were engaged in such activity, only a few truly understood the contents of what they were copying. What was this '*dag-yig*'? What was this '*sum-cu-pa*'? Nobody knew the answers and no one knew whom to ask. Several students didn't even know how to say the titles, *Dag-yig* and *Sum-cu-pa*, when they wanted to borrow these texts. All of this resulted in some laughable situations. On one occasion, a student wanted to borrow a text from his friend:

'Aro! I just finished making a notebook. Could you lend me something to copy?'

'Sure. Which book do you want? *Quotations from Chairman Mao?*' His friend teased him as usual.

Not realising that his friend was joking, the student replied, 'No. No. I already have *Quotations from Chairman Mao*. There are some books called *Rjes-'jug* [suffix] and *Sngon-'jug* [prefix].'

'Gosh. I don't have either of those. But I do have a book called *Bar-'jug* [literally, middle-fix].' The friend continued teasing him.

Still the boy didn't get the joke. '*Bar-'jug. Bar-'jug.* Uhm.' He thought for a moment and said, 'OK then. This *Bar-'jug* should be all right. Please lend me that.'

His name was Chodpa, but ever since he borrowed that book we always called him 'Bar-'jug.'

One evening when we had finished dinner and an hour remained before the night study session, a small group of students were in our room, some writing in their copy books, some cutting paper, others playing the board game Go. Suddenly, the school bell rang. If it rang once it meant class was over. Twice meant class was starting. And three times signalled an urgent announcement. That night it rang three times, and then a fourth. And still it continued to ring.

These were the times of greatest risk, when a teacher might burst into our room to summon us. We worried not about what had happened outside, but that a teacher might enter our room and see us making the spelling and grammar books. We hesitated, not knowing where to hide what we had been copying. We didn't want to hide them under the beds. We could hide them under the mattresses, but that didn't seem safe. We were especially uncomfortable about hiding them in the

Drepung monastery, 1990: Chinese graffiti obliterate sacred Buddhist murals.
Credit: © P. Collinson / Tibet Images

mattress stuffing, the memory of the *la-gzhas* collection confiscated from inside the coverlet of a fellow student still fresh in our minds.

'Oh! I've got it. It'll be all right,' one of us exclaimed. We turned and saw the boy looking up towards the ceiling. We too looked at the ceiling. Everything *would* be all right! There was a good-sized hole in the ceiling. The first of us to see the opening climbed on to a fellow student's shoulders. We passed all the original books and our copies up to him, and he slid them into the opening. But one student hesitated.

'Quick! Hand it over! We've got to get out of here soon,' I urged him anxiously.

'If we saw that hole, the teachers will notice it as well. Right?' he observed.

This sobered us. He was right, we thought. But there was nothing we could do and we were out of ideas.

'Hurry up! Get to the meeting hall. What are you doing in there? Didn't you hear the bell?!' Someone was yelling outside; and the bell was still ringing.

The one student jumped down from the other's shoulders and raced outside. The boy who hadn't hidden his books stuck them into the back of his pants and ran out with the rest of us.

By the time we reached the hall, the other teachers and students had already assembled but the meeting had not yet started. Students were talking among themselves and there was a terrible clamour. As soon as we had filed into one of the rows and taken our seats, we heard the strident voice of the convenor:

'All rise!' The din in the hall stopped short, as if cut by a knife. We stood and turned our faces towards the portrait of Mao Zedong.

'"The East is Red". And one . . . And two . . .' The leader called out. Again the hall filled with sound. This time, however, it was a noise less likely to fade away – the sound of one hundred voices singing in unison.

We sang 'The East is Red', made supplications for the long life and prosperity of Mao Zedong and Lin Biao, and recited passages from *Quotations from Chairman Mao*. Though these preliminaries lasted no longer than on previous occasions, they seemed interminable that day.

At last they came to an end and we took our seats. The hall again fell quiet. Everyone was waiting for some unlucky fellow to approach the podium, hat in hand, with his head bowed to the audience.

Before spotting any such person, however, we heard a voice. It was our principal. He held up a book. 'What is this?' he demanded, displaying it for all the hall to see. This was no ordinary book. It was small and wrapped in red paper. Though we couldn't make out the title, it was obviously written in gold lettering. Students seated in the front rows of the hall responded without hesitation: 'That's *Quotations from Chairman Mao!*' they cried. Those of us in the middle and back rows echoed this response in a succession of voices.

'Look carefully! Is this really *Quotations from Chairman Mao*?' The principal queried, raising the book even higher.

We again waited for the students in the front rows to answer, but they remained silent.

'If one looks at the cover of this book, it is *Quotations from Chairman Mao*. However . . .' The principal opened the book and showed it to us. 'Look! These are not the quotations of Chairman Mao on the inside!'

Those of us in the back half of the hall could see nothing but the white of the pages; not a single word was visible. Yet the students in front could apparently see what was written there. They looked at each other and began to whisper. The hall was soon buzzing with murmurs.

'Look!' The principal shouted again. 'Look! Poisonous weeds have been hidden between the covers of *Quotations from Chairman Mao*. Here is some *dag-yig* [spelling]. And here we have some *sum-cu-pa* [grammar].

And look! There is more!' Meanwhile, he was flipping through the book and showing random pages to the hall.

'And, finally, what do we have here?'

Yes, what *was* this last section? The students were anxious to know. It seemed that even those in the front rows couldn't see what it was. Frozen to attention, they stared at the book in the principal's hand.

After a momentary glance, the principal recited: '*Pretty little cuckoo bird, singing on the mountaintop* . . . Could Chairman Mao have spoken such words? You tell me! How would it be if revolutionary leaders and revolutionary teachers tricked you like this? What should we be reading during our Daily Study? *Quotations from Chairman Mao* or love songs and poisonous weeds?!'

The principal continued his interrogation, answering every question himself.

'Oh, Blessed Buddha!' I thought. 'This student was so clever! Oops. I mean to say, what a terrible crime he has committed! Who was this person? How would he be punished? I don't see any police, so maybe he won't be arrested. Or perhaps he's already been arrested and taken to prison.' These questions and fears flooded into my mind. Though I saw the principal's mouth moving, I didn't hear a word he said.

Finally, I brought my attention back to what the principal was saying. It turned out the book belonged to a student named Haunde Gya. He had already escaped from school about two months ago when teachers found out that he had stolen some notebooks and ink from one of the offices. It was rumoured he hadn't even returned home. There was no one to punish.

Nevertheless, the principal carried on with his lecture: The poisonous weeds of 'cow's-demons and snake-spirits' were growing among the students. Though the school authorities already knew who was making such copybooks, if the guilty students admitted to their mistake by handing over the poisonous weeds, they would be exonerated. On the other hand, failure to turn in the books would result in severe punishment. After a long string of such threats, the meeting was adjourned. ❑

Pema Bhum *left Tibet for India in 1988 where he founded a Tibetan literary magazine and newspaper. He now lives in New York. The above excerpt is from* Six Stars with a Crooked Neck. *Translated by Lauren Hatley*

SUSANNAH SHEFFER

Beyond retribution

Despite the prevailing sentiment in the USA, not every victim of murder claims revenge: some of the victims' families have learned that death row is no answer to their grief

It's a striking sight: about 40 people crowded on to a small stage, looking out at the audience. One after the other they speak, saying their names and then the name of the member of their family who was murdered. We hear of mothers, fathers, sons, daughters, sisters, brothers, grandparents. Each statement contains an entire horror, a story the speakers are not telling now but the impact of which is palpable behind their words. Each speaker adds after this, 'And I oppose the death penalty.'

The members of Murder Victims' Families for Reconciliation are unusual in the United States. In a country that has executed 682 people since the death penalty was reinstated in 1976 and has about 3,800 sitting on death row today, most people assume murder victims' families are crying out for executions. Prosecutors seeking the death penalty righteously claim to be seeking justice for the grieving families and giving them what they want and need. If you happen to be opposing the death penalty on some other grounds – its racism, its cost, its failure to deter – inevitably the person taking the other side of the argument will offer what they believe is the ultimate challenge: 'But what if someone in *your* family were murdered? How would you feel then?'

When Renny Cushing talks about how he felt after his father was murdered, he uses phrases like 'emotionally filleted'. He talks about the searing shock, the emptiness, the incomprehension. The idea that his father would open the door of his home one ordinary June evening and be greeted by a shotgun blast which would rip his chest apart in front of his wife of 37 years – how could Renny possibly have imagined this. How could he have imagined touching the blood on his father's face as he lay on the hospital gurney. Or going to the telephone and trying to find words to tell his brothers and sisters that their father had just been

Renny Cushing

murdered for no reason they could fathom. Or standing with his mother
in the hospital room, seeing her reach into her pocket for a tissue and
coming up with a packet of seeds that she'd put there that morning
when she and her husband were planting their garden, the spring ritual
they cherished every year. 'I won't be needing these any more,' she said,
already envisioning the ways that her life would be for ever diminished
by this loss.

The pain of that night is a pain that will mark the surviving Cushings
for ever. When you talk to Renny now, 12 years after the murder, you
can see that in some way he is still trying to figure out how to bear
it. But one thing he has known from the beginning is that pain
isn't something you can get rid of by transferring it to someone else.
'Sometimes people think it's a zero-sum game,' he says. 'They think if

Bud Welch

they can make someone else feel pain, theirs will go away. I just don't think it works that way.'

Renny's interest in reducing violence, rather than adding to it, not only means that he opposes the death penalty. It also means that when he ran into the son of his father's murderer outside the courthouse one day, he understood that nothing would be gained by having that son lose a father too. 'I knew that to kill somebody else not only wouldn't honour my father's life; it would create another grieving family.'

It took some time, but Bud Welch was able to come to the same realisation. Bud's daughter Julie Marie was killed in the bombing of the Oklahoma City Federal Building in April 1995. When Bud travels the country and tells about the day, audiences are drawn into one particular heart of a tragedy that they felt vividly, and in some sense collectively, when it originally took place. Bud talks about how wrecked he felt after the bombing, how strong was his desire to retaliate by killing Timothy McVeigh and Terry Nichols – the convicted bombers – himself. When he learned that President Clinton and Attorney General Reno would seek the death penalty, he looked forward to it, 'because here I had been crushed, I had been hurt, and that was the big fix'.

What do you do with the hurting? For weeks Bud smoked too much, drank too much, felt what he now recalls as a kind of temporary insanity. Then, about nine months after the bombing, he went down to the place where it happened and stood under an old American elm that had survived that April day. He let his mind wander to the upcoming trials and the likely executions, and he said to himself, 'How's that going to help me? It isn't going to bring Julie back.' He realised that the death penalty 'is all about revenge and hate, and revenge and hate is why Julie and 167 others are dead today.' Gradually, Bud realised that he didn't want the killers executed. Before long, he was making his viewpoint publicly known.

If pain *were* a zero-sum game, Bud might have felt better when he saw McVeigh's father on television and saw in his eyes a look of devastation that reminded him of his own. But when he went to visit Bill McVeigh and sat around his kitchen table for an hour and a half, it was not to try to increase anyone else's suffering or even to lessen his own. It was simply to sit there as two fathers, with the pain between them.

It's hard to find a word for this. It's something like reconciliation, though not necessarily in the sense of forgiving and certainly not with any element of forgetting. It is something like saying, a terrible thing happened and I cannot go back so I have to find a way to keep walking, wounds and all.

The more time one spends with families of murder victims, the deeper is one's sense that what is wanted, maybe even more than revenge, is recognition and acknowledgement of the harm done. Vengeance says *that'll show him*, and it may be the desire to show that is really most primary – the desire to speak the truth of one's pain and have it met with acknowledgement.

Paula Kurland, whose daughter Mitzi was raped and murdered by Jonathan Nobles, participated in Texas's Victim-Offender Reconciliation programme, where she was given the opportunity to meet with Nobles while he awaited execution on death row. She approached the meeting carrying a photograph of her daughter, and explained to the television reporter who was following the event, 'Jonathan is going to see what he took.'

They sat across from each other for two hours, separated by glass, and what Jonathan was forced to do in those hours was see – see what he took, see what he had done. At the end of the visit we hear Jonathan say, 'I tried to change my life in prison and it's not enough, nothing will ever be enough, but I *am* sorry.' By the time the two put their hands up to the glass in prison's makeshift handshake, we sense that they have both seen something. Tears run down Jonathan's face as he listens to Paula, but he doesn't turn away. 'The sight of his own crimes is the highest agony a man can know,' wrote Arthur Miller. Maybe it is. Yet unlike the pain of further violence, this agony of acknowledgement and recognition seems somehow redemptive, or at least part way towards healing.

That's how it seems in Randy Reeves's letter to Gus and Audrey Lamm. Reeves, a Native American who was adopted as a young boy by a Quaker family, was convicted of murdering Janet Mesner and Victoria Lamm in a Meeting House in Nebraksa in 1980. He was sentenced to die, and as the date of the execution drew near, family members of both victims were among those speaking out against it. When Reeves wrote a letter to Victoria's husband Gus and their daughter Audrey (who had been only two at the time of the murder), he believed they would be receiving it after his death. He told them that their actions on his behalf brought Victoria alive to him in a way that nothing had before. The letter does not ask for anything, but speaks simply of Reeves's shame and sorrow.

Reeves received a stay of execution, and Gus and Audrey Lamm continue to fight for his life. They believe that's what Victoria would have wanted, and they, too, feel that nothing would be gained by causing further suffering. 'I know what misery is,' Gus says, 'and I don't want that misery spread around. There's enough misery in the world already.'

Soon after receiving the letter, Gus was able to visit Reeves in prison. 'I wanted to let him know that I didn't hate him. I hated what he did, and I hated the prolonged nightmare that my life had become. When the murder first happened, I wanted to see him as some type of monster, but the more I learned about him, the more tragic a figure he appeared to me. And now I didn't want to see him as either a monster or a cause I was fighting for – I wanted to see him as a human being. He looked me in the eye, which is more than the governor of Nebraska ever did.' Trying to speak with the Governor about his views, Gus had been frustrated by the man's unwillingness to meet his eyes, and had repeatedly asked him for that courtesy as he spoke.

Execution is attractive because it seems to match the original horror, to exact measure for measure. It seems a way of doing something. It must have been this impulse that led a friend of the Cushing family to say to Renny, as he passed him in the supermarket soon after his father's murderers had been apprehended, 'I hope they fry those people so your family can have some peace.'

Yet peace and comfort may actually consist of something quite different. The hardest thing for a society to accept may be that some wounds cannot close, not all the way. What we need to learn how to do may be in some ways more difficult than offering retribution. Writer and psychotherapist Lauren Slater writes: 'Sometimes all we can do is align ourselves with the wound ... Sometimes all we can do is keep company with the person who hurts.' What is necessary, Slater says, is simply 'to acknowledge pain, to sit still in its mysterious power and feel helpless.'

Maybe we need to learn to keep company with the pain that murder causes. Not minimising it, not trying to displace it, but aligning ourselves with it so that in time some truly helpful responses might become apparent, or some ideas about preventing it from happening again, so that when survivors stand before us and speak of their loss, we are able to meet their gaze, feel its impact and not look away. ❏

Susannah Sheffer is writer-in-residence at Murder Victims' Families for Reconciliation and is working on In a Dark Time: A Prisoner's Struggle for Healing and Change

SARAH A SMITH

Disappearing Turks

Bulgaria is something of an unknown quantity in the West: still a land of red wine and poisoned umbrella tips. Yet the Bulgarian government has high hopes that tourism will boost the country's economy. Whether or not their expectations are realistic, and save for a few gaps in the narrative, there is historical splendour and natural beauty in abundance

If there is one thing missing for the traveller in Bulgaria, it is any sense of the country's Ottoman past. The centuries of Ottoman rule (1393–1878) are portrayed as Bulgaria's dark ages. In signs and explanations from Rila monastery in the south-west to the capital Sofia's grandiose National History Museum, this period, generally rounded up to 500 years, is one of 'slavery' under the 'Turkish yoke'. This emotive, nationalistic spirit takes stone form at the Freedom Monument, the tower which commemorates the decisive victory over the Turks at Shipka Pass. Situated on the top of Mount Stoletov, the monument can be seen for miles from the surrounding plains, and it is here that we begin to understand how historical hatreds can be kept alive.

In the National History Museum we find Thracian gold, icons and church artefacts, treasures from the first and second kingdoms. We see nothing Islamic, no Ottoman craftsmanship, or certainly nothing described as such, and ask ourselves: what have they done with 500 years? Where has it all gone? Even the term Ottoman seems dangerous: after I have rashly uttered the word in public my brother, a resident of Sofia, tells me that it is not really a name to use here. For Bulgaria, 1876, the year of the April uprising which marked the beginning of the final and very bloody struggle for liberation, seems to be a kind of year zero.

We first glimpse the level of esteem in which Bulgarians hold their Ottoman past in Veliko Tarnovo, the capital of the second kingdom, in the east of the Balkan range. In the remains of Tsarevets, the ruined citadel, we find what appear to be turban-headed Ottoman tombstones. They lie smashed and discarded, a rubble of sculpted masonry. No one seems remotely interested in them and they are not deemed museum-worthy.

Under communism, it wasn't just Ottoman relics that suffered but the ethnic Turkish minority – another fragment of empire. Turkish town and village names were Bulgarianised in 1940. Fierce campaigns, first in 1972 and then from 1984, to make Turks adopt Bulgarian names led to clashes in which at least 50 Turks were killed. Muslim traditions were discouraged, mosques closed down and speaking Turkish in public was prohibited. It is hardly surprising that, when given the chance to emigrate, thousands of Bulgarian Turks participated in the 'Great Excursion' to Turkey which started in the summer of 1989.

Veliko Tarnovo, Bulgaria: Ottoman remains.
Credit: Sarah A Smith

Krassimira Popova, a freelance journalist based in London, tells me that Bulgaria is now much more open about its past, if not especially interested in it. 'The Turkish issue is very old,' she says. 'For Bulgarians today the most important thing is their savings accounts and the economic level of the country.'

Ayla Redjeb, a primary school English teacher from the ethnic Turkish stronghold of Kardzhali in southern Bulgaria, responds similarly when I ask her about her community's feelings: 'We will never forget what happened, but we won't live in the past . . . we must look to the future.' Ayla still feels the effects of communist policy, however. Turks (8–9% of the population) face discrimination in the job market, she says, and some of her colleagues treat her badly. And there is often friction between Turks and Bulgarians before elections: 'Turks vote for the Movement for Rights and Freedom [the de facto party of the ethnic Turks] but Bulgarians are against it. They say they don't want to be governed by a Turkish party.'

Some of the tensions between Bulgarians and Turks, and the Turkish struggle for status, are evident when we look at the country's mosques. Our first attempt to visit one is a disappointment and a shock. Stopping off at Stara Zagora, the 'old town behind the mountain', we decide to visit Eski Dzhamiya (Old Mosque), built in 1409. A relaxed, urbane town of long boulevards and a sprawling central park, Stara Zagora has a certain café-culture chic. It's a place to stroll but, as it turns out, it's not a place for mosques.

The guidebook admires Eski Dzhamiya's 17-metre-wide dome and promises an interesting inscription within. But the guidebook is out of date. The large dome on the squat building is indeed impressive, but we can't get in to see the inscription. I realise this before we reach the dilapidated, weed-strewn porch because a café-cum-bar has attached itself to a corner of the building, like a large, impudent limpet. Its long list of cocktails is hardly a sight for an imam's eyes. At the mosque's entrance, clearly abandoned for several years, lumps of concrete have been dumped in the porch and the windows and doors are boarded up.

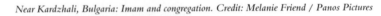

Near Kardzhali, Bulgaria: Imam and congregation. Credit: Melanie Friend / Panos Pictures

A swastika and the word 'Nazi' sprayed
beside the door warn me off.

We find our first functioning mosque
in Plovdiv, the country's second city and
a draw for businessmen and tourists alike.
We approach it with some trepidation:
my brother says they are a target for local
skinheads (as are synagogues). We edge our
way through the gate of Plovdiv's Imaret
Dzhamiya, built in 1444 and situated a little
way from the main thoroughfares. Imaret
Dzhamiya has a fine minaret of zigzagging
brickwork and four bemused, rather
rumpled-looking old men and three shyly
smiling old women sit on guard outside. We
stumble to take off our shoes before we even
open the door – an unnecessary precaution,
the sentinels signal to us. Our sandals join
a small and rather poignant collection of
presumably abandoned shoes – there is no one inside and they don't
belong to the sentinels.

*Imaret Dzyamiya, Plovdiv: poor
but loved by its congregation.
Credit: Charles Hunnewell*

There are other surprises. Imaret Dzhamiya's prayer hall is poor.
It is less a faded and shabby reminder of past glories than a chipped,
fragmented ruin of them. Around the whitewashed dome are patches,
never bigger than a foot square, of wall paintings: blue and red patterns
curling briefly along the curve of the roof and then disappearing
abruptly. There are about four of them. It is a fascinating hint of the
richness there once was and of the link between the Byzantine church
paintings I've seen here, which it recalls in pigment, and the Islamic
tradition. But it's only a hint.

At eye level, the interior, obviously cared for to the best of the
congregation's means, offers a slightly brighter face. There are banners
of Kufic script, gold on green. A huge photograph, dating from the early
20th century, presents the Kaaba in the Haram mosque at Mecca. This
is clearly not a place without love: as we stand an old woman hurries
in and over to the mihrab. She flicks a switch and a string of bright,
white fairy lights snap on, illuminating the otherwise bare prayer
niche. Incongruous, even gaudy, the lights do add a touch of hope.

At least the Imaret is open and visibly in use. Dzhumaya Dzhamiya (1359–85) 'the Friday mosque', is open only on the Muslim sabbath and feast days. The sign on its nearly concealed door promises more extensive opening times, but experience proves otherwise and recent travellers confirm that they too could not find out when it really opens.

Attention has clearly been lavished on the Dzhumaya. On the edge of Plovdiv's main street and not far from the rambling cobbled streets of the tourist-haunted old town, its exterior brickwork has been renovated. More work is planned: following a visit to Plovdiv in July the mayor of Istanbul suggested a joint restoration project, with Istanbul municipality supplying the finance and expertise and Plovdiv the administration. Tourist stalls of woodwork and postcards run along one side of the building, but this is an edifice to be proud of. Or one side of it is. The main entrance is another matter. Shops and a pizza parlour have been stuck on to the front of the building, obscuring not just design but purpose. The entrance, up a steep, narrow flight of stairs, between parlour and shop, is easily missed by a casual wanderer and seems secondary to the commerce below. It is a surprise to see the sculpted, painted doorway crammed in like a secret between modern buildings.

Sofia's Banya Bashi mosque, built in 1576, stands on Boulevard Kryaymiya Mariya Luiza, its thin minaret rising proudly into the sky. It is just across from TSUM, formerly a Soviet-style department store and, opposite, the old market hall or Hali. Both TSUM and the Hali have undergone recent, radical renovation into smart, western shopping emporia. The Hali reopened in May 2000 after many years, a hopeful sign for Bulgaria's economy.

As far as I can tell, Banya Bashi hasn't had a revamp. Stalls selling soft drinks, tapes of folk-pop and magazines line the exterior, as if providing the building with a disguise. The entrance is easy to miss. The mosque hardly looks open; the iron gate stands ajar but that is the only sign of activity. No sentinels gesture us in here, and our visit feels somehow furtive. Maybe it's a throwback to worse times. Under communism, visiting any place of worship was an activity you'd want to keep secret – while religion was never stamped upon in Bulgaria in the same way that it was in the Soviet Union, attending a church or mosque was a poor career move. Since 1989, Bulgaria's churches have undergone a revival and visiting any number of chapels we see people of all ages queuing for candles, teachers kissing icons and their charges following suit.

Sofia, Bulgaria: Banya Bashi mosque struggles against radical consumerism. Credit: Sue Hunnewell

Muhammad clearly hasn't been so lucky. It's Friday, but the prayer hall of Banya Bashi is empty save for a bored-looking caretaker, slumped at the foot of the minbar, and a research student from Senegal. Thrilled to see visitors, he stops pacing with his prayer beads and greets us. This, he tells us, is the only working mosque in Sofia. In neighbouring Macedonia's capital, Skopje, he notes, there are ten. It may be the capital's only mosque (another, the nine-domed Buyish Djami or Big Mosque, built in 1494, is now home to the National Archaeological Museum), but Banya Bashi's prayer hall makes an effort. The creamy dome is decorated with freshly painted, curling blue patterns, the walls adorned with banners, there is a flash of silver here and there, the mihrab is carved, if undecorated. The muezzin is rumoured to sound here, though we never hear him. He is, apparently, quite quiet. ❑

Sarah A Smith *is a freelance journalist based in London*

NEW FROM VERSO . . .

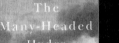

A NEW GENERATION DRAWS THE LINE
Kosovo, East Timor and the Standards of the West
NOAM CHOMSKY

'One of the West's most influential intellectuals in the cause of peace.'
The Independent

1 85984 789 7   hardback   £16

THE MANY-HEADED HYDRA
The Hidden History of the Revolutionary Atlantic
PETER LINEBAUGH AND MARCUS REDIKER

'For most readers the tale told here will be completely new. For those
already well aquatinted with the seventeenth and eighteenth centuries,
the image of that age which they have been so carefully taught and
cultivated will be profoundly challenged.'
David Montgomery

1 85984 798 6   hardback   £19

LATE VICTORIAN HOLOCAUSTS
El Nino Famines and the Making of the Third World
MIKE DAVIS

'This is first-rate history . . . A major contribution to understanding how
capitalists used the vagaries of the climate to create underdevelopment
in the late-nineteenth-century
world.' *Immanuel Wallerstein*

1 85984 739 0   hardback   £20

EHUD'S DAGGER
Class Struggle in the English Revolution
JAMES HOLSTUN

'Powerfully cogent, often brilliant in its stylistic sophistication, and
magisterial in the range of its scholarship . . . a work brimming with
intelligence.' *Chris Fitter, Rutgers University*

1 85984 782 X   hardback   £25

AVAILABLE AT ALL GOOD BOOKSHOPS
Verso UK, 6 Meard Street, London W1F 0EG • Tel 020 7437 3546
Verso US, 180 Varick Street, New York, NY 10014-4606 • Tel 212 807 9680
email: publicity@verso.co.uk • www.versobooks.com

VERSO